CommonSense Grammar and English for Professionals

by

Phillip S. Sparks

Copyright 2008
by
Phillip S. Sparks
Nashville, Tennessee

ISBN 978-0-9819172-8-3

All rights reserved. No part of this publication may be reproduced or transmitted in any form or by any means, electronic or mechanical, including photocopy, recording, or any information storage and retrieval system, without permission in writing from the author.

PREFACE

Four or five hundred years ago, a single human being could know everything worth knowing. This ideal Renaissance man or woman studied medicine, law, philosophy, and the arts, often excelling in each of these fields. Alas, such simple times have passed.

We are now immersed in a revolution. Technological advances and the unshackled creativity of democratic societies have given birth to a new era, the information age. No one alive would dare lay claim to all knowledge worth knowing.

Today, most of us specialize. We dedicate years of learning and productivity to a single field. Air travel, computer programming, banking, and countless other activities are made possible by scores of specialists, each doing what few others know how to do.

Specialists form a chain of expertise that binds our complex society together, but they provide only every second link of the chain. The alternate links represent the specialist's ability to communicate with others. Unless these professionals can communicate effectively, their expertise is of little value.

CommonSense Grammar and Style was written with the business professional in mind. It will help you, the professional, write better letters and memorandums. It will help you avoid common errors, organize your messages, express yourself clearly, and find more information when you need it. It will teach you the basic survival skills.

The emphasis in ***CommonSense Grammar and Style*** is always on simplicity. When several approaches to a common problem are possible, this book presents the least complicated and the most consistent. If you follow its advice, you will be on safe ground, but you must realize that other good writers may choose other correct solutions.

Do not be deceived. Neither this book nor any other book will make you an instant authority in business writing. It can provide nothing more than a foundation. You will spend the rest of your life building on that foundation.

Please keep in mind that *CommonSense Grammar and Style* was written specifically for the business world. If you are a technical writer, a journalist, an academician, or a creative writer, you will find it helpful, but you must remember that certain rules and guidelines taught here apply only to business writers.

CommonSense Grammar and Style relies on *Merriam-Webster's Collegiate Dictionary* (called "Merriam-Webster") for the spelling of words and abbreviations. Merriam-Webster is widely recognized as the American standard.

In matters of usage, especially business usage, *CommonSense Grammar and Style* depends heavily on *The Gregg Reference Manual* (called *Gregg*) by William A. Sabin. Careful readers will, however, notice occasional differences between the two. For example, *Gregg* ignores Merriam-Webster's simplification of abbreviations while this book welcomes it, and *Gregg* does not object to the use of data as a singular noun. This book does.

Such minor disagreements cannot diminish my profound respect for *Gregg*. It is the best single resource available to business writers.

CommonSense Grammar and Style has been in the making since 1987. It has grown from a 20-page booklet to its present form. I am grateful to a number of people who have made it possible. The administrators at Nashville State Technical Institute, especially Bill Johnson and Richard Jenkins, have been extremely cooperative, and my loving, patient wife Kitty has always understood.

The greatest debt, however, is owed to my students. Their requests account for the addition of numerous chapters, and their suggestions have improved countless passages. They have also been delightfully persistent in helping me ferret out errors. Indeed, this book is dedicated to my students. I have learned far more from them than they have learned from me.

CommonSense Grammar and Style will be in a state of revision as long as I live. If you have suggestions, corrections, or other comments, please write. I will acknowledge every contribution.

Phillip S. Sparks
2020 Claylick Road
White Bluff, TN 37187

CONTENTS

1 Subject-Verb Agreement 1
2 Pronouns 7
3 Four Comma Rules 13
4 The Semicolon 25
5 Colons and Dashes 27
6 Capitalization 29
7 Numbers 31
8 *Who* or *Whom*, *Whoever* or *Whomever* 35
9 Abbreviations 43
10 Comparatives and Superlatives 45
11 Plurals 47
12 Possessives 51
13 Frequently Misused Words 57
14 Spelling 65
15 Hyphenating Compound Adjectives 69
16 The Subjunctive 77
17 Active Voice versus Passive Voice 83
18 The Business Style: Simple Clarity 87
19 Emphasizing Important Information 99
20 Organizing Letters 103
21 Special Letters 111
22 Proofreading Skills 119
23 Improving Your English 121
24 Reference Books 123
   APPENDIX A: PRETEST 125
   APPENDIX B: ANSWERS TO THE EXERCISES 147
   INDEX 169

HAVE YOU CONSIDERED TAKING THE PRETEST?

If *CommonSense Grammar and Style* is new to you, you may want to take the pretest in "Appendix A."

The pretest can help you decide which chapters you need to study.

AS YOU DO THE EXERCISES IN THIS BOOK CHECK YOUR ANSWERS IN "APPENDIX B: ANSWERS TO THE EXERCISES"

Check each of your answers before you go on to the next item.

Checking your answers as you go will allow you to profit from your mistakes.

1 SUBJECT-VERB AGREEMENT

1:01   "Subject-verb agreement" is a fancy term for a simple idea: The subject and the verb must work together.

> **PRACTICE 1-A**
> Underline the subjects and circle the correct verbs.
> 1. John (are, is) the new director.
> 2. Those men (work, works) on Mondays.
> 3. The herd (was, were) well managed.

In the first sentence, we easily recognize that John is the subject and *is* is the verb. The subject, John, "agrees with" the verb *is*. To say "John *are* the new director" would violate subject-verb agreement. Similarly, we confidently select men *work* and herd *was*.

WHAT ARE VERBS?
Most verbs (The italicized words) show action (*make*, *walk*, *live*, etc).

>He *built* the house all by himself.
>She *ran* the course in 31 minutes.

Some verbs describe the way things are (*is*, *seem*, *feel*, etc).
>They *were* early.
>Sue *looks* much better.

Other verbs express ownership (*have*, *own*, *want*, etc).
>The car *has* a new transmission.
>That tank *contains* oxygen.

Sometimes, verbs are several words long.
>Wanda *has been working* there five years.
>Someone *will have to go* to the office.

WHAT ARE SUBJECTS?
The subject is the person or thing that *acts*, *is*, or *owns*. Most subjects (like all of the underlined words above) stand immediately in front of the verb.

Frequently, other words separate the subject from the verb.
>Several of them still *use* slide rules.
>A group of trainees *is* in the classroom.

Occasionally, the subject follows the verb.
>There *were* three applicants.
>On the wall *hung* two medieval swords.
>*Are* you going to the fair?

The subject can be **the understood you**.
>*Take* my car. (You *take* my car.)
>*Turn* it on after you *plug* it in. (You *Turn* it on after you *plug* it in.)

PRACTICE 1-B
First, find and circle the verb. Next, underline the subject.

1. The steps collapsed.
2. Someone in Personnel wrote the letter.
3. Don't forget the instruments.
4. My cousin is the CEO.
5. The CEO is my cousin.
6. My train will be late.
7. Her assistant needs a new printer.
8. Jeff feels more confident now.
9. Glenda and Roy will be married next month.
10. She owns and manages a small business.
11. Is the train from Berlin on time?
12. Somewhere in California lives a woman with 22 children.
13. Please ask Tina about the books.
14. They are going to announce his promotion.
15. Her car was parked by the door.

(See Appendix B to check your work when the answers are not given in the text.)

Most of the time, we use correct subject-verb agreement without giving it a thought. At times, however, even careful writers violate subject-verb agreement. That happens most often when one of the following five situations complicate matters.

1. WHEN INFORMATION FALLS BETWEEN THE SUBJECT AND THE VERB

1:02 Information between the subject and the verb can cause confusion.

The list of clients *were* mailed yesterday.

This example is incorrect because *were* should be *was*. The subject of the sentence is list, and the list *was* mailed yesterday. The prepositional phrase "of clients" confused the person who made this mistake. Admittedly, the mistake is unlikely because it's impossible to mail clients. In the following exercise, such errors may be harder to avoid.

PRACTICE 1-C
First, circle the correct verb. Next, underline the subject.

1. The herd of wild horses (was, were) well managed.
2. That set of instructions (need, needs) to be revised.
3. A group of excited school children (are, is) eagerly awaiting the blastoff.

In the first sentence, you might think "wild horses" is the subject and mistakenly choose *were*, but "wild horses" can't be the subject because it's in a prepositional phrase. The subject is herd, and the herd *was* well managed. In the second sentence, we might think instructions *need*, but set *needs* is correct. "Instructions" is in a prepositional phrase and can't serve as the subject. In the third sentence, group, not "children," is the subject, so we must choose *is*.

As more information is inserted between the subject and the verb, making subjects and verbs agree becomes increasingly difficult.

PRACTICE 1-D
First, circle the correct verb. Next, underline the subject.
1. The type of programs we use to monitor our accounts (are, is) complex.
2. A team of surgeons from six hospitals in three states (was, were) there.
3. By dusk, a flight of mallards with 12 drakes and 14 hens (was, were) on the pond.

When you write long, complex sentences, check the subject-verb agreement carefully. Don't let prepositional phrases and other intervening words confuse you.

1:03 NOTE: Usually, the subject of the sentence, not a prepositional phrase, determines the verb form. The subject and the verb agree while prepositional phrases are ignored. In a few special cases, however, prepositional phrases can control subject-verb agreement.

At least four indefinite pronouns, *all*, *some*, *none*, and *any*, can be singular or plural depending on the prepositional phrases that follow them. Certain nouns, like *most*, *plenty*, and *percent*, also depend on prepositional phrases to make them singular or plural.

All of the wood *is* burning, and all of the pots *are* steaming. (wood = singular, pots = plural)

None of the damage *is* serious, and none of the men *are* hurt. (damage = singular, men = plural)

Is any of the cake missing, and *are* any of the candies gone? (cake = singular, candies = plural)

Plenty of sugar *is* available, and plenty of eggs *are* in the basket. (sugar = singular, eggs = plural)

Only 28 percent of the wheat crop *was* harvested, but 93 percent of the melons *were* sold.
 (wheat crop = singular, melons = plural)

Other such words are *a lot*, *enough*, *part*, *percentage*, *rest*, and *total*. The word *Number* can also be singular or plural. *The number* is singular while *a number* is plural. (The number of visitors *is* impressive though a number of them *are* leaving.)

PRACTICE 1-E
First, circle the correct verbs. Next, underline the subjects as well as the prepositional phrases that make them singular or plural.
1. (Are, Is) any of the food hot, and (are, is) any of the tables set?
2. None of the parts (was, were) worn, but none of the work (has, have) been done.
3. Plenty of tickets (are, is) available, and plenty of space (are, is) left.

2. WHEN UNUSUAL WORDS FORM PLURALS WITHOUT AN S
1:04 Many words form plurals that don't end with an *s*. (See 11:13.) A few examples are *children*, *mice*, *deer*, *oxen*, *feet*, *teeth*, *geese*, and *fish*. We easily recognize such plurals because we use them often, but when uncommon words form their plurals without adding *s*, we often mistakenly treat them as singular nouns.

The word *data* is plural. The singular is *datum*. Since *data* doesn't end with *s*, we often see this mistake:

The data *is* incorrect.

The subject-verb agreement is also incorrect. *Is* should be changed to *are*.

The data *are* incorrect.

Similar problems occur with words like *media* (*medium* is singular), *alumni* (*alumnus* is singular), *syllabi* (*syllabus* is singular), and *criteria* (*criterion* is singular).

PRACTICE 1-F
First, circle the correct verb. Next, underline the subject.
1. The bacteria (are, is) extremely dangerous.
2. The parenthesis (print, prints) too far to the left.
3. The nuclei (was, were) much larger an hour ago.

Don't take chances with such unusual words. Check your dictionary.

3. WHEN *OR* OR *NOR* SEPARATES TWO OR MORE ELEMENTS IN THE SUBJECT

1:05 When the subject of a sentence is made up of two or more elements joined by the word *and*, we easily choose the correct verb.

The twins **and** Mr. Pulaski *are* coming over.

If we replace *and* with *or* or *nor*, we are more likely to make a mistake. The element *closest to the verb* should be in charge of the subject-verb agreement.

Either the twins **or** Mr. Pulaski *is* coming over. (Think "Mr. Pulaski *is*.")

Neither the twins **nor** Mr. Pulaski *is* coming over. (Think "Mr. Pulaski *is*.")

but

Either Mr. Pulaski **or** the twins *are* coming over. (Think "The twins *are*.")

Neither Mr. Pulaski **nor** the twins *are* coming over. (Think "The twins *are*.")

PRACTICE 1-G
First, underline the critical word in the subject. Next, circle the correct verb.
1. Neither Carol nor her brothers (want, wants) to go.
2. Either the backpacks or the canoe (are, is) too heavy.
3. Neither the company cars nor one of the company trucks (was, were) used.

When you use *or* or *nor*, double-check the subject-verb agreement.

4. WHEN THE SUBJECT COMES AFTER THE VERB

1:06 In most sentences, the subject comes first, and the verb follows it.

Two men *are* inside.

Sometimes, however, the verb precedes the subject.

There *are* two men inside.

When the verb precedes the subject, people make mistakes similar to these examples:

There*'s* two reasons we need to meet.

To the left of the bridge *is* five new I beams.

Actually, both sentences should use *are*.

In the first, <u>two reasons</u> *are*.

In the second, <u>five new I beams</u> *are*. (Try reading it "There *are* <u>five new I beams</u>.")

PRACTICE 1-H
First, circle the correct verb. Next, underline the subject.
1. There (was, were) several people involved.
2. Beyond those trees (live, lives) an old badger.
3. Out by the fence in the lumber yard (are, is) several thousand bricks.

We make these errors more frequently in conversation than in writing, but all too often, our spoken mistakes find their way into our writing.

5. WHEN VERBS END WITH *ST*

When we pronounce words like *resists* and *costs*, we tend to slide over the final *s*. When we do, "These days, that computer *costs* $10,000" sounds like "These days, that computer *cost_* $10,000."

If we stop writing the *s*, the spoken slur becomes a written error. Be careful with verbs that end in *st*.

PRACTICE 1-I
Underline the subjects and circle the correct verbs.
1. Her brother (fast, fasts) every third day.
2. That ledger (list, lists) all the companies we currently serve.
3. The plan (consist, consists) of hundreds of steps.

Add *s* to these verbs whenever you would add *s* to verbs like *work* and *run*. (It works, it runs, it co*sts*)

EXERCISE 1
SUBJECT-VERB AGREEMENT
STEP 1: Circle the correct verb.

STEP 2: Underline the subject that controls the verb you circled. If a subject can be singular or plural, underline the subject *and* preposition phrase that makes it singular or plural.

EXAMPLE: Here (*are*, is) <u>two examples</u> of her photography.

1. The data from England (are, is) the most reliable.
2. The book about King George III, the revolution, and the British navy, (are, is) destined to become a classic.
3. There (are, is) numerous variables involved here.
4. An eagle (nest, nests) in this area.
5. The size of the computers used in the labs (are, is) yet to be determined.
6. Beyond the large oaks in those vacant lots (lie, lies) the foundation of the old roundhouse.
7. Try to stop any logs or trash that (come, comes) down the river.

8. The news media (are, is) going to be there.

9. Enough of us (was, were) there, so we held the meeting.

10. The collection of photographs (are, is) in the desk.

11. The group of visitors (are, is) waiting in the parking lot.

12. Underneath those boxes (are, is) an assortment of textbooks.

13. The alumnus (are, is) on the committee.

14. This year, a new house (cost, costs) less than it did last year.

15. The vertebra (was, were) not broken.

16. In the windows of all the shops in town (sit, sits) the tiny doll that Martha designed.

17. The paint that the men used to redecorate the offices (has, have) a seven-year guarantee.

18. A lot of fungi (are, is) needed to keep our lab running smoothly.

19. Either some accountants or a group of boys (are, is) scheduled to answer the phones.

20. The type of fertilizers that they use (are, is) highly effective.

21. In the areas we manage, there (are, is) ample potential for growth.

22. His syllabi (was, were) highly detailed.

23. The discussion held by our engineers, designers, and executives (are, is) bound to improve productivity.

24. There (are, is) several reasons our profits are so high.

25. The news from the reporters on the islands (are, is) keeping hope alive.

26. If the coach (contest, contests) that ruling, we may win.

27. Neither the conductor nor the violinists (want, wants) to postpone the concert.

28. The cacti in her garden (are, is) from New Mexico.

29. Down by the river (are, is) two boats we can rent.

30. Currently, this tree (cast, casts) a shadow over her flower garden.

31. Either Mr. Maddox or his sisters (has, have) agreed to bring the food.

32. This batch of English muffins (look, looks) much better than the last one.

33. The suspect (insist, insists) that she is innocent.

34. A flock of geese (has, have) set up housekeeping out by our pond.

35. The nuclei (has, have) an equal number of neutrons and protons.

2 PRONOUNS

2:01   As with subject-verb agreement, pronouns seldom cause problems, but five cases deserve our attention. A sixth case will be of interest to conservative writers.

1. WHEN ANOTHER NOUN OR PRONOUN CAUSES CONFUSION

2:02   People often become confused and select the wrong pronoun when they use one pronoun with another noun or pronoun.

> They ordered the new desks for *he* and *I* (incorrect).

> *Me* (incorrect) and my brother will fly to New York.

We can easily pick the correct pronoun if we simplify the situation by temporarily dropping the other nouns or pronouns from the sentence.

> They ordered the desk for *him* (not *he*). They ordered the desk for *me* (not *I*). They ordered the new desks for *him* and *me* (correct).

> My brother will fly to New York. *I* (not me) will fly to New York. My brother and *I* (correct) will fly to New York.

2:03   NOTE: Grammatical courtesy requires that we place other people's names (and the pronouns that represent them) first. Never write "I and my brother" or "me and him." Always list yourself last.

> **PRACTICE 2-A**
> Correct the following sentences.
> 1. Karl and her live in Atlanta.
> 2. Are you and him looking for Connie?
> 3. Me and Sonia will ride with she and Bill.

When you correct sentence 3, grammatical courtesy requires you to write ***Sonia and I.*** The other pair can be written ***her and Bill*** or ***Bill and her***. Both are correct.

2. PRONOUNS WITH *AS* OR *THAN*

2:04   People often choose the wrong pronoun when it follows *as* or *than*.

> She can read better than *me* (incorrect).

> Bill isn't as tall as *her* (incorrect).

We can easily pick the correct pronoun if we continue the sentence to include the next verb. The sentence also sounds more natural when we add the verb.

> She can read better than *I* (can).

> Bill isn't as tall as *she* (is).

NOTE: Compare "She likes chocolate better than me" ("She would rather eat chocolate than spend time with me.") with "She likes chocolate better than I (do)." The meanings are quite different.

7

PRACTICE 2-B

Correct the following sentences.
1. She can dance far better than him.
2. Chang is at least as qualified as her.
3. I'll bet I'm stronger than him.

3. REFLEXIVE PRONOUNS

People often have trouble with reflexive pronouns. (Reflexive pronouns end with *-self* or *-selves*.)

Yesterday, I bought *me* a new raincoat. (Incorrect. Use *myself*.)

They organized *theirselves* into a team. (Incorrect. Use *themselves*.)

The Governor asked Mr. Worthington and *myself* to intercede. (Incorrect. Use *me*.)

Reflexive pronouns look back to a noun or pronoun already used in the sentence. Never use a reflexive pronoun unless the word it represents precedes it.

I ⟼ myself	*I myself* installed the new water heater.
you ⟼ yourself	Watch *yourself*. (The *you* is "understood.")
he ⟼ himself	*He* (*Russ*) never caught *himself* making that mistake again.
she ⟼ herself	*She* (*Lynn*) felt *herself* sinking.
it ⟼ itself	*It* (*The dog*) found its way home all by *itself*.
we ⟼ ourselves	*We* (*Floyd and I*) shook *ourselves* and crawled out of the car.
you ⟼ yourselves	*You* (*You and Carol*) can fix it all by *yourselves*.
they ⟼ themselves	*They* (*The Chiltons*) described *themselves* as experienced contractors.

NOTE: Never use *hisself* or *theirselves*. They are not standard English.

PRACTICE 2-C

Correct the following sentences.
1. The Queen sent Robert and myself a letter of gratitude.
2. He hurt hisself working with a chain saw.
3. Using his stationery, I wrote me a first-rate letter of recommendation.

4. PRONOUNS WITH *-ING* WORDS

People often use the wrong pronoun in front of *-ing* words.

I appreciate *you* (incorrect) *helping* us proofread that report.

Compare the preceding example with the following sentence:

I appreciate *your advice*, I appreciate *your support*, and I appreciate *your help*.

Helping, like **advice**, **support**, and **help**, is a noun (a thing), and the pronoun in front of it must be possessive.

I appreciate *your* (correct) *helping* us proofread that report.

Here are some more examples. In each case, the *-ing* word represents *something* (a noun).

Our (not *Us*) winning the contest surprised them all. (*What* surprised them? *Something*.)

I deserve credit for *your* (not *you*) *being* first. (*What* do I deserve credit for? *Something*.)

His (not *Him*) playing the piano was the high point of the evening. (*What* was the high point of the evening? *Something*.)

PRACTICE 2-D
Correct the following sentences.

1. Them flying to Vancouver was my idea.
2. We admired him kicking the ball with such accuracy.
3. You agreeing to come with us encouraged everyone involved.

NOTE: When you name the person or thing instead of using a pronoun, keep using the possessive form.

1. Ian and Gordon's flying to Vancouver was my idea. (See 12:13.)
2. We admired Joe's kicking the ball with such accuracy.
3. The CEO's agreeing to come with us encouraged everyone involved.

In a few cases, the possessive pronoun would be the wrong choice. Here is an example:

We saw *him* painting the apartment. (*Whom* did you see? *A person*.)
but
We saw *his* painting the apartment as a gesture of goodwill. (*What* did you see as a gesture of goodwill? *Something*.)

Use a possessive pronoun only when the statement answers the question *what*. When the question is *who* or *whom*, don't use a possessive pronoun.

5. *THEM* USED TO REPLACE *THESE* OR *THOSE*

Never use *them* to replace *these* or *those*.

Those (not *Them*) people just won't give up.

PRACTICE 2-E
Correct the following sentences.

1. Them trucks are ready to roll.
2. Why won't you let them kids ride the pony?

NOTE: Using *them* to replace *these* or *those*, like using *ain't*, could mark you as an uneducated person.

6. SINGULAR PRONOUNS USED WITH *THEY, THEIR,* AND *THEM*

People often use the plural pronouns *they*, *their*, and *them* when the gender (sex) of a singular noun or pronoun is unknown. Here is an example:

No one brought *their* (incorrect?) text to class today.

No one is singular and *their* is plural. Strictly speaking, this sentence is incorrect.

Many authorities now say that such sentences use a standard idiom (idioms are illogical expressions the linguistic community accepts as correct, and our language has many idioms). In fact, only conservative grammarians object to this usage. If your approach to our language is conservative, read on.

2:12 *Everyone, anyone, no one, everybody, anybody, nobody*, and *each* are always singular. Masculine pronouns like *he* and *his* (sometimes called *masculine unisex pronouns*) are used with these words to represent both males and females unless the group is mainly or entirely female (mothers, actresses, etc).

No one brought *his* (correct) text to class today.

Although the sentence is now correct, most careful writers consider his to be sexist. We can avoid such sexist language three ways.

2:13   1. Instead of *he*, use *he or she*. Instead of *him* use *him or her*. Instead of *his*, use *his or her*.

No one brought *his or her* (correct) text to class today.

Unfortunately, the frequent repetition of *his or her, him or her*, and *he or she* is awkward.

2:14   2. Reword the sentence to avoid the sexist pronoun.

No one brought *the* text to class today.

The is neither sexist nor awkward.

2:15   3. Replace the pronoun at the beginning of the sentence with a plural pronoun.

None of the students brought *their* (correct) text to class today.

NOTE: Remember that *all, some, none*, and *any* are special pronouns. They can be singular or plural. When one of these words represents a single object, it's singular. When it represents more than one, it's plural. For example, *none* of the bread *was* missing, and *none* of the dishes *were* dirty. (See 1:03.)

PRACTICE 2-F
Consider the following sentence.

If anyone calls, tell *them* that *they* can leave *their* message with Sue.

a. Why is this sentence incorrect?

b. Correct is using the masculine unisex pronoun.

c. Use dual (masculine and feminine) pronouns.

d. Revise the sentence to make the plural pronouns correct.

e. Rewrite the sentence to avoid the troublesome pronouns.

EXERCISE 2
PRONOUNS

I. Circle the correct pronouns, and make sure they fall in the proper order.

1. Can anyone here run as fast as **(her, herself, she)**?

2. In addition to **(me, myself)**, John was honored.

3. She is certain that he approved of **(me, my, myself)** applying for the position.

4. When I'm depressed, I go shopping and buy **(me, myself)** a book.

5. None of **(them, those)** students were more motivated than **(her, herself, she)**.

6. The director talked to Mary and **(he, him, himself)** about the paper.

7. He thinks that **(their, them)** appealing to the Supreme Court will be a waste of time.

8. The elderly man planted the corn all by **(himself, hisself)**.

9. **(I, Me, Myself)** and Bill are going to the movies.

10. **(Him, His)** having worked here before helped him win the promotion.

11. The candy was a gift for Sarah and **(I, me, myself)**.

12. He isn't as quick as Roger or **(I, me, myself)**.

13. We encourage **(you, your)** taking time off to work in the community.

14. Those applicants are better prepared than **(ourselves, us, we)**.

15. The clerk and **(her, herself, she)** cleaned up the mess.

16. My brother is far more cautious than **(her, herself, she)**.

17. The three officers saw **(him, his)** leaving the restaurant.

18. Please make sure that either Sam or **(her, herself, she)** signs the receipt.

19. She doesn't approve of **(you, your, yourself)** allowing Beverly to read the report.

20. Nobody here can rope a calf as skillfully as **(he, him, himself)**.

21. Go ahead and address the package to **(me, myself)**.

22. Richard and **(he, him, himself)** purchased the pens for **(I, me, myself)** and Joe.

23. **(Them, Those)** monkeys often fight among **(theirselves, themselves)**.

24. **(Their, Them)** asking for a raise had nothing to do with it.

25. **(He, Him)** and **(her, she)** enjoy talking to **(I, me)** and Roger.

2:17 II. (For Conservatives Only) Sentences 1, 2, and 3 misuse *they*, *their*, or *them*. Review 2:11 through 2:15, and attack each problem sentence by:

   a. Stating why the sentences are incorrect
   b. Correcting them using the masculine unisex pronoun
   c. Correcting them using dual (masculine and feminine) pronouns
   d. Revising them so that the plural pronouns will be correct
   e. Rewriting them to avoid the troublesome pronouns

   EXAMPLE: Did anyone at the meeting forget their briefcase?

   a. *Anyone* is singular and *their* is plural. Both should be singular or both should be plural.

   b. Did *anyone* at the meeting forget *his* briefcase?

   c. Did *anyone* at the meeting forget *his or her* briefcase?

   d. Did *any of the people* (plural) at the meeting forget *their* briefcase?

   e. Did *anyone* at the meeting forget *a* briefcase?

   1. Everyone remembered to bring their checkbook.

      a.
      b.
      c.
      d.
      e.

   2. A nurse can make more money if they work weekends.

      a.
      b.
      c.
      d.
      e.

   3. Not one of the employees was stopped if they were wearing their photo ID.

      a.
      b.
      c.
      d.
      e.

2:18 NOTE: Most good conservative writers prefer solutions *d* and *e*. They are neither sexist nor awkward, and they obey the rules of traditional grammar. At least one of them, *d* or *e*, is likely to fit any situation.

3 FOUR COMMA RULES

3:01 Commas cause more trouble than any other aspect of English usage. The rules in this chapter don't cover all uses of commas, but they do treat the four areas where most errors occur.

To understand commas, we must understand basic sentence structure. The standard sentence is an independent clause with the subject in position one and the verb in position two. The remaining information follows the verb. Here are three typical independent clauses:

<u>John</u> *is* a good mechanic.

<u>He</u> *refuses* to charge for the work he does.

Check all the drawings carefully. (The subject is **the understood <u>you</u>**.)

Think of an independent clause as a group of words that could stand alone as a simple sentence.

Commas signal a departure from this standard structure. Recognizing independent clauses is the key to using commas correctly.

RULE ONE

3:02 Use a comma when a coordinating conjunction joins two independent clauses. The six coordinating conjunctions are **and, but, or, nor, yet**, and **so**.

<u>INDEPENDENT CLAUSE</u>, *coordinating conjunction* <u>INDEPENDENT CLAUSE</u>.

<u>John is a good mechanic</u>, *but* <u>he refuses to charge for the work he does</u>.

3:03 When *both* of the independent clauses are short (four words or fewer [See 3:28.]), many good writers drop this comma. We will call it optional.

<u>The parts are here</u>, *and* <u>the drawings are done</u>. (This comma is optional.)

3:04 CAUTION: Do not use a comma unless you do, in fact, have two independent clauses. In the following example, the part of the sentence after *but* can't stand alone as a sentence.

<u>John is a good mechanic</u> *but* refuses to charge for the work he does.

3:05 Sometimes, coordinating conjunctions join three or more independent clauses.

<u>Make sure the parts are in stock</u>, *and* <u>check all the drawings carefully</u>, *but* <u>don't start production until we hear from headquarters</u>.

In the preceding sentence, the subject of each independent clause is **the understood <u>you</u>**.

PRACTICE 3-A
Underline the independent clauses and fill in the commas.
1. They processed your order today so you should receive it by Monday.
2. The interstates are almost impassable and the airport is closed due to high winds so our auditor might not be here tomorrow.

3. Bill cut the wood and Mary loaded it.
4. Add milk and butter to the flour but don't add salt at this point.
5. She saved for years so that her children could go to college.

3:06 NOTE: Sentence 5 does not take a comma because *so that* is not a coordinating conjunction. Do not confuse *so* with *so that*. *So* means "therefore." *So that* means "in order that."

They processed your order today, *so* (therefore) you should receive it by Monday.
but
She saved for years *so that* (in order that) her children could go to college.

We frequently drop the *that* in *so that*.

She saved for years *so* her children could go to college.

This *so* still means "in order that." Don't add a comma when you drop the *that* from *so that*. *So* means "therefore." *So that* means "in order that," even when the *that* is understood but not written.

RULE TWO
3:07 Use commas when introductory elements stand in front of the independent clause.

Introductory element, INDEPENDENT CLAUSE.

As we approached the entrance to the bank, we heard a loud explosion.

3:08 When the introductory element is short (four words or fewer [See 3:28.]), the comma is optional. If we hear a pause after a short introductory element, we are more likely to use a comma.

By Tuesday, we should be in Moscow. (This comma is optional.)

3:09 Remember that introductory elements always precede the independent clause. Consider these two examples:

First, Susan must learn to read. (This comma is optional.)

While walking along the beach, she discovered several interesting footprints.

When we move the introductory element to the middle or back of the independent clause, the Rule Two comma disappears. The following sentences don't need commas.

Susan must *first* learn to read.

She discovered several interesting footprints *while walking along the beach.*

3:10 Sometimes a sentence with a Rule One comma in it has an introductory element in front of the second independent clause. These Rule Two commas are exceptionally difficult to spot.

Her ship took her to Bimini, (Rule One) and *while walking along the beach,* (Rule Two) she discovered several interesting footprints.

PRACTICE 3-B
Underline the independent clauses and fill in the commas.

1. If the storm strikes during the night they won't stand a chance.
2. Her mind stopped wandering as soon as the nurse called her name.
3. Coughing and wheezing the child trailed after his mother.
4. On the road to Zanzibar she made her fortune and lost her soul.
5. In the Outback sheep are the key to survival.
6. After four days of hard work they cleared the old mine shaft and with cheers and shouting all around he was taken to the hospital.

RULE THREE

3:11   Use commas to separate three or more items in a series.

A, B, and *C*

The series usually falls inside an independent clause.

> They bought him *a hat, a coat,* and *a new pair of shoes*.
>
> She enjoys *working in the garden, playing cards,* and *watching television*.

A series can be made up of independent clauses.

> *Alfred is in France, Wilson is dead,* and *Ralph has simply disappeared*.

A series can also lie outside the independent clause.

> *By Tuesday, Wednesday,* or *Thursday*, we should be in Moscow.

The comma after *Thursday* is a Rule Two comma.

3:12   NOTE: Most journalists and some academic writers drop the last comma in a series, the one before the conjunction, but the experts in business writing recommend that we keep it.

3:13   Rule Three also applies to a series of two or more adjectives. When two or more adjectives precede a noun, place a comma between the adjectives.

adj, adj NOUN

Insert a comma between the adjectives if you could have used *and* in place of the comma.

> We moved her *big*, (and) *soft*, (and) *fluffy* SOFA into the *bright*, (and) *colorful* ROOM.

If you do, in fact, add *and*, drop the comma.

3:14   At times, you might be tempted to use a RULE THREE comma between two adjectives when the comma does not belong there.

> Her cute, lovable puppy wore a leather, dog collar.

Check these commas by replacing them with the word *and.*

> Her cute *and* lovable puppy wore a leather *and* dog collar.

When *and* fits, the comma is correct. When it doesn't, the comma is incorrect. In this example, the comma after *cute* is correct, but the comma after *leather* isn't.

PRACTICE 3-C
Underline the independent clauses and fill in the commas.

1. She chopped the onions peeled the potatoes and carefully added the spices.
2. The computer is too old the walls need to be painted and the rent is a bit high.
3. A deck of cards a bottle a bath a week and freedom from labor were all he ever wanted.
4. In January April July and October new quarterly reports will be issued.
5. He ran a small unprofitable business for two years fought as a mercenary for one year and spent the rest of his short turbulent life taming crocodiles.

3:15 NOTE: When a comma subdivides each item in a series, replace the Rule Three commas with semicolons. (See 4:05.)

RULE FOUR
Rule Four commas set off interrupters. First we will cover the basic rule. Then we will examine how Rule Four works with dates and states.

3:16 **THE BASIC RULE FOUR**
Use commas to set off a word or group of words that *clearly interrupts* a sentence.

THIS SENTENCE, *interrupter*, USES NORMAL SENTENCE STRUCTURE.

Claire sat down, *humming softly*, and watched the fire fighters lose their battle.

Will Rogers, *the cowboy philosopher*, never met anyone he didn't like.

Humming softly clearly interrupts the first example. *The cowboy philosopher* clearly interrupts the second.

Remember, the word or group of words must *clearly interrupt* the sentence. Are the commas in this sentence correct?

A woman, who worked here last year, is running for mayor.

No. *Who worked here last year* DOES NOT clearly interrupt the sentence. The average reader would not pause between *woman* and *who*. The commas must be removed. To qualify for Rule Four, a word or group of words must *clearly interrupt* the sentence.

3:17 An interrupter usually falls inside a sentence, but it can fall at the end of a sentence, often sounding like an afterthought.

THIS SENTENCE USES NORMAL SENTENCE STRUCTURE, *afterthought.*

Claire sat down on the curb, *humming softly*.

Her grandfather knew Will Rogers, *the cowboy philosopher*.

Danny couldn't break the eight-minute mile, *not even the ten-minute mile*.

English for Professionals

3:18 An interrupter can also fall inside an introductory element.

When Steve Morris, *Chuck's supervisor*, left, Chuck applied for his job.

After Shelia talked to her supervisor, *Martha Plumber,* Shelia decided to apply too.

The comma after *Plumber* is working for two masters, Rule Two and Rule Four.

PRACTICE 3-D
Underline the independent clauses and fill in the commas.

1. Little Patsy who had never been to town before followed her brother everywhere.
2. Computers unlike people are fast and accurate.
3. Lee Howard talked to Sid Norman our vice president and solved the problem.
4. Her accounts are with the oldest bank in town Planters' Trust.
5. When we ordered the book the one he recommended we also bought a new pen.

RULE FOUR WITH DATES AND STATES

3:19 When you write the month, day, and year, treat the year as an interrupter.

She started working there on *January 13, 1940,* and retired on *October 1, 1970.*

3:20 When the day of the week precedes the date, treat both the month-day unit and the year as interrupters.

We set sail on *Tuesday, July 28, 1993,* and reached Boston on *Thursday, September 2.*

3:21 NOTE: No comma is needed when only the month and year are given.

The flood occurred in *December 1903* and was followed by two tornados.

3:22 If you use the international format for dates, treat the day, month, and year as a single unit.

She started working here on *13 January 1940* and retired on *1 October 1970.*

We set sail on *Tuesday, 28 July 1993*, and reached Boston on *Thursday, 2 September.*

3:23 When a state or country follows the city, treat the state or country as an interrupter.

He flew from *Nashville, Tennessee*, to *London, England*, in only six hours.

PRACTICE 3-E
Underline the independent clauses and fill in the commas.

1. He reached Lima on December 28 1942 and crossed into Colombia the following Sunday January 3 1943.
2. He reached Lima on 28 December 1942 and crossed into Colombia the following Sunday 3 January 1943.
3. We drove to Augusta Maine in June 1984 to check on our investments.

NOTE: Does the punctuation go inside or outside closing quotation marks?

3:24   Commas and periods *always* go inside.

He said, "Those stocks are overvalued," and she told him to "Sell them immediately."

3:25   Question marks and exclamation marks go inside closing quotation marks when they belong to the material being quoted. Otherwise, they go outside.

I clearly remember her asking me, "Have you ordered the maps*?*"

Did you hear him say that "The report must be in by Wednesday"*?*

3:26   Colons and semicolons always go outside closing quotation marks.

We hired the following "technicians": a janitor, a cook, and a plumber.

3:27   **SUMMARY**
You may find it convenient to refer to this summary as you work through the following exercises.

RULE ONE
INDEPENDENT CLAUSE, *coordinating conjunction* INDEPENDENT CLAUSE.
   The coordinating conjunctions are **and, but, or, nor, yet,** and **so** (but not **so that**).
   Rule One commas are optional if *both* independent clauses are short (four words or fewer).

RULE TWO
Introductory element, INDEPENDENT CLAUSE.
   Rule Two commas are optional if the introductory element is short (four words or fewer).

RULE THREE
A, B, and **C**
also
adj, adj NOUN (Put a comma between these adjectives if you could have used *and*.)

RULE FOUR
THIS SENTENCE, *interrupter*, USES NORMAL SENTENCE STRUCTURE.
or
THIS SENTENCE USES NORMAL SENTENCE STRUCTURE, *afterthought*.
   To qualify for Rule Four, the word or group of words must *clearly interrupt* the sentence.

3:28   NOTE: Throughout this book a *short* phrase is defined as "four words or fewer." **Long** is "five or more words." These definitions are, of course, arbitrary, but they simplify matters. When you have finished working with this book, you may redefine *short* and *long* to suit yourself.

English for Professionals   19

3:29   **EXERCISE 3a**
       COMMAS
       Underline the independent clauses and add the missing commas. *Fill in all "optional" commas and circle them.* In the space above the commas, write the numbers of the rules that justify your corrections.

       CAUTION: You may skip sentences 26 through 35. They are exceptionally difficult.

   1. Darryl helped Jose write a résumé and Joyce helped him compose the cover letter.
   2. The van was rented this morning and the pickup truck is in the shop but we still have several station wagons.
   3. Sheila arrived this morning but Steve flew in yesterday.
   4. Take good notes and let me know whether the new program will affect our division's responsibilities.
   5. Dorothy completed the letter by noon and mailed it during her lunch break.
   6. They leased more office space so that they could hire six new employees.
   7. We left an hour early so we wouldn't have to deal with rush hour traffic.
   8. She didn't sign out so she must still be in the immediate area.
   9. In order to keep his appointment he left for work an hour early.
   10. We must purchase three printers but if they offer us a professional discount we will go ahead and order five.
   11. Within one hour we had interviewed four applicants.
   12. We worked all weekend and by Monday morning the report was in the mail.
   13. We need to add envelopes labels and pens to the shopping list.
   14. They want to read your analysis study the contract and review our proposals before they schedule a meeting.
   15. The desks are in the warehouse the chairs are on the truck and the mattresses are on the loading dock.
   16. A tall well-dressed woman met us at the door.
   17. Our last mail clerk the one you met at the reception was promoted and was transferred to Palo Alto California.
   18. Our office has a new computer the very model you recommended.
   19. The auction started at 9 AM on Tuesday May 10 1995 and ended the following Wednesday afternoon.
   20. If the lawyers the accountants and the labor leaders can work out the agreement we will start production by the end of the year.
   21. Most of our money is in mutual funds.

22. Our division managers including Dorothy Charlie and Lee are eager to work out a simple effective compromise.

23. Payroll taxes income taxes and users' fees have reduced our income so we must find a way to operate more profitably.

24. In some cases we work directly with the manufacturers but most of the time we have to go through wholesale dealers.

25. By the time we had completed our long exhaustive study we knew we had to cut costs expand operations or find new markets.

26. Their briefing on advances in computer technology the one you heard in Boston was well planned well presented and highly informative.

27. The steel beams are in place but without the safety belts the ones OSHA requires we can't continue working.

28. The business he founded as a young man made him a millionaire and allowed him to pay for the education of all four of his children and all ten of his grandchildren.

29. Sometimes the well-drilling equipment breaks down and on those occasions we call Crossville Pennsylvania to order parts.

30. When they bought the new hard drive for the computer the PC in Shirley's office they should have bought a new printer a new monitor and a new keyboard.

31. If the invoice arrives send me a copy of it and tell the supervisor in the warehouse to treat the shipment with care.

32. He sent me a short well-written memorandum dealing with two important topics employee morale and continuing education.

33. We signed a four-year contract for $5 million.

34. Our counterparts in France have requested that we try to work out a simple method for keeping them supplied with raw materials and equipment so that they can avoid costly shutdowns and layoffs.

35. Punctuation skills like math skills are developed through long repetitive drills and with patience anyone can learn to punctuate correctly.

English for Professionals 21

3:30 **EXERCISE 3b**
COMMAS
Underline the independent clauses and add the missing commas. *Fill in all "optional" commas and circle them.* In the space above the commas, write the numbers of the rules that justify your corrections.

CAUTION: You may skip sentences 26 through 35. They are exceptionally difficult.

1. If the weather is warm enough he wears T-shirts to work.

2. Richard replaced a knob adjusted the fine tuning and tightened two nuts.

3. In spite of the loud banging noises they slept but none of them slept well.

4. Gail hung the curtains and with the help of friends we moved the sofa in.

5. Monday my uncle the one who lives uptown came by to see us.

6. Charles will leave next Thursday March 15.

7. Margaret spoke with the members of the board three days before she decided to announce her resignation to the public.

8. We can order now or we can wait.

9. Occasionally Ms. Collins our night dispatcher works the morning shift.

10. They completed the house yet the final project the landscaping had to be postponed.

11. Whenever he came to town he stopped for coffee at the Colonial Inn.

12. We worked all day on the budget but could not come up with the money for a new computer.

13. We have similar goals so you don't have to worry about cooperation.

14. Though she had never been on a horse she dressed cursed and drank like a cowhand.

15. When the auditor found two serious perplexing discrepancies we had to revise our procedures.

16. Our buyer is in Salem Massachusetts for a show and the manager is in Seattle Washington attending a conference but the manager's assistant will be glad to talk to you.

17. After a short stint in the Army however he took a job with the CIA.

18. Show her the program documentation but don't let her enter the computer center.

19. By noon they were in Chicago but no one was there to meet them.

20. The treaty was signed on 31 March 1992 and as you can see we all live in peace.

21. The trucks the materials and the crews are ready so we should start work tomorrow.

22. He won the battle but she won the war.

23. She left Brussels Belgium on December 14 1956.

24. A technician from the computer shop on Third and Walnut repaired my computer so that it now works as well as a new one.

25. Wait for gold prices to drop and invest your excess cash in mutual funds.

26. When Sue went to Europe Carla Norma and Pam her three best friends traveled with her.

27. Back then the demand for plastics was limited so profits were low but now we can't keep up with the orders.

28. When I talked to Bill our contact in Reno he said Alfred is at fault but I think Carol Smothers their assistant mailed us the wrong bill.

29. In spite of the confusion the students the faculty and the administrators met and the conflicts at least the critical ones were resolved.

30. When we ask him to write letters run errands or file he acts as if he is being rewarded.

31. Sometimes she feels left out especially when we go to lunch without her.

32. Although she graduated she never looked for a job and her grandparents parents and brothers still support her.

33. The lights in the work area must be replaced because they are too intense and create unnecessary eye fatigue.

34. Although Katharine was new her supervisor the chief accountant trained her well and after only two weeks she felt like an experienced employee.

35. That big mean ugly Hell's Angel is Carol's date and her rich stuffy father is upset.

English for Professionals

3:31 **EXERCISE 3c**
COMMAS

Underline the independent clauses and add the missing commas. *Fill in all "optional" commas and circle them*. In the space above the commas, write the numbers of the rules that justify your corrections.

CAUTION: You may skip sentences 26 through 35. They are exceptionally difficult.

1. If you want to write better letters learn to proofread carefully.

2. He was brilliant but without a dictionary he couldn't spell his own name.

3. In terms of structure passive voice and active voice are completely different.

4. Capitalization can be tricky but if you proofread carefully and follow a few simple guidelines you will seldom make errors.

5. Years ago stilted phrases fancy words with little meaning were commonly used in business writing.

6. The most important "special letter" is the letter of application.

7. Letters of recommendation are also extremely important because you could slow the advancement of a friend's career if you don't know how to write a good one.

8. Specific language emphasizes information but general language de-emphasizes it.

9. Occasionally the bad news the statement of refusal should be in the opening sentence.

10. Euphemisms can help us deal with painful or distasteful matters but clichés overworked words and phrases interfere with communication.

11. When your letter must say *NO* try to write it without saying *NO* and always maintain respect for your reader.

12. Goofy reading pronouncing each syllable with the same dull tone is an excellent way to proofread.

13. *Fowler* is an excellent book on usage and is now available in paperback.

14. Don't apologize for saying *NO* not unless the problem is your fault.

15. Since most people mispronounce *prerogative* they also misspell it.

16. Roger will drive and Sharon will take notes.

17. After she practiced using *lie* and *lay* for two weeks she began to choose the correct word unconsciously.

18. Use active voice most of the time and try to avoid noun piles.

19. To defend his position he hid behind company policy and his letter was a flop.

20. *Ain't* is nonstandard English and if you keep using it you could hurt your chances for a successful career.

21. The *reals gets* and *verys* have been cleaned out so the language in our report sounds much fresher.

22. She wrote the letter so that he could concentrate on his report.

23. He did it.

24. Mr. D. R. Swanson met with the president this afternoon and agreed to write the guidelines that will describe our company's preferred formats for letters and memorandums.

25. Write him another letter saying *NO* and this time use the direct approach.

26. When closing a bad-news letter use resale offer an alternative refer confidently to future business relations or take more than one of these approaches.

27. If you have to deny credit however do your best to keep the applicant as a cash customer and eventually that person could become a trusted client.

28. Rule One commas are easy to use and Rules Three and Four seldom cause trouble but Rule Two commas cause more problems than all the others combined.

29. In spite of the mistake the manager the clerk and he behaved like gentlemen and they solved their problems at least the important ones.

30. When a group of words can stand alone as a simple sentence it's called an independent clause.

31. The fastest way to proofread effectively is to combine two strategies goofy reading and reading with a straightedge.

32. Although she wrote several letters of application she did a sloppy job and neither CBS NBC nor ABC invited her in for an interview.

33. Semicolons may be used in complex sentences to replace certain commas but are not commonly used to separate independent clauses or to add afterthoughts.

34. He wrote a short polite letter with good word variety good sentence variety and plenty of white space.

35. In spite of her lack of experience Jane the owner's daughter was given the job but after only two weeks she resigned and eagerly returned to college.

4 THE SEMICOLON

4:01 The semicolon is a hybrid, part period and part comma. It's weaker than a period but stronger than a comma.

Today, many careful business writers avoid semicolons. This chapter shows you how to use semicolons and how to avoid most of them.

1. SEMICOLONS AS STRONG COMMAS

A. SEMICOLONS AND RULE ONE COMMAS

4:02 You may use a semicolon (as a strong Rule One comma [See 3:02.]) when a coordinating conjunction joins two independent clauses *if* one or both of the clauses use Rule Two, Rule Three, or Rule Four commas.

> Ted, my supervisor, works on the tenth floor; but I work on the ninth.

4:03 Several years ago, the semicolon would have been required. Today, most good business writers downgrade this semicolon to a normal Rule One comma.

> Ted, my supervisor, works on the tenth floor, but I work on the ninth.

4:04 NOTE: Most journalists and many other good writers upgrade this semicolon to a period and capitalize the coordinating conjunction.

> Ted, my supervisor, works on the tenth floor. But I work on the ninth.

If you follow their lead, be aware that starting a sentence with a coordinating conjunction offends some conservative writers.

B. SEMICOLONS AND RULE THREE COMMAS

4:05 When a comma subdivides each item in a series, replace the Rule Three commas with semicolons.

> Her area includes Augusta, Maine; Montpelier, Vermont; and Concord, New Hampshire.

> He traveled to New York on July 3, 1990; August 2, 1991; and June 9, 1992.

This semicolon is the only semicolon most good business writers still use.

2. SEMICOLONS AS WEAK PERIODS

4:06 You may use a semicolon (as a weak period) between two closely related independent clauses that are not joined by a coordinating conjunction.

> John and Mary work on the fourth floor; the meeting will be held in the basement where we keep last year's files.

4:07 Most good business writers would use a period instead (or we could add a coordinating conjunction and use a Rule One comma). This semicolon becomes more nearly acceptable as the independent clauses become shorter and more closely related.

> John works on the fourth floor; Mary works on the ninth.

Still, a period would work as well, and most good business writers prefer the period.

3. SEMICOLONS WITH TRANSITIONAL EXPRESSIONS

4:08 You may use a semicolon (as a weak period) between two independent clauses if a conjunctive adverb joins them. *The Gregg Reference Manual* groups conjunctive adverbs with similar phrases and refers to them all as "transitional expressions." Here are some examples:

accordingly	*consequently*	*for example*	*furthermore*
meanwhile	*however*	*in fact*	*nevertheless*
on the contrary	*otherwise*	*therefore*	*then*

We all work on the fourth floor; ***nevertheless***, the meeting will be held in the basement.

4:09 Most careful business writers replace this semicolon with a period, allowing the transitional expression to start the next sentence. The comma after the transitional expression becomes a Rule Two comma. These expressions are short, but the Rule Two comma is not optional. (See 3:08.)

We all work on the fourth floor. ***Nevertheless***, the meeting will be held in the basement.

4:10 NOTE: Whether we use semicolons or periods in front of transitional expressions, a comma usually follows the transitional expression. The exception is the transitional expression ***then***.

We had lunch; then we went to the station.
or
We had lunch. Then we went to the station.

4:11 Semicolons are used to construct long, complex sentences. The trend in business writing is toward simple clarity. Consider avoiding almost all semicolons.

4:12 **EXERCISE 4**
SEMICOLONS
Step 1: Add the missing semicolons (and the missing commas).
Step 2: Show how most good business writers would avoid most of the semicolons.
1. Howard, the junior partner, will be in charge but he won't make any major decisions.
2. They have lived in Pueblo Colorado Santa Fe New Mexico and El Paso Texas.
3. Sarah thought we were upset with her on the contrary we think she has made excellent progress.
4. Ms. Simms is highly competitive I'm not.
5. We didn't expect to win all of our games however we did expect to win the tournament.
6. Commodities prices are rising rapidly for example the last two weeks have seen the price of wheat increase more than 30 percent.
7. Before he applied to IBM, he took his civil service exam and he seriously considered a career with the Department of Labor, the Department of Commerce, or the FBI.
8. The training sessions are scheduled for Tuesday November 6 Thursday November 15 and Monday December 3.
9. They bought their farm several years before Honda picked the site for a plant then they sold it for a considerable profit.
10. She invited Gil, Sandra, George, and Sam and Ralph invited me.

4:13 NOTE: If you revised sentence 10 by placing a semicolon after ***Sam***, you improved its clarity. If you then replaced the semicolon with a comma, you made it harder to understand. How can you avoid the semicolon and preserve clarity?

5 COLONS AND DASHES

5:01 Many people find colons and dashes confusing. The rules in this chapter will help you use them correctly.

COLONS WITH LISTS IN SENTENCES

5:02 Use a colon at the end of an independent clause that introduces a list. The list usually has at least three items. If it opens with a transitional expression like *for example*, a comma is placed after the transitional expression.

<u>The committee has four new members</u>: ***Karen, Will, Thomas, and Walter.***
<u>Our apartments offer many convenient features</u>: ***for example, covered parking, patio balconies, and energy-efficient appliances.*** (Notice that a comma falls after *for example*.)

5:03 CAUTION: Do not use the colon unless an independent clause precedes it. The following sentence uses a colon incorrectly:

The four new committee members are: ***Karen, Will, Thomas, and Walter.***

To correct this sentence, drop the colon.

The four new committee members are ***Karen, Will, Thomas, and Walter.***

COLONS WITH LISTS IN COLUMNS

Currently, there are few widely accepted rules for punctuating information arranged in columns. The following guidelines are simple and reasonable and will bring consistency to your work.

5:04 Use a colon after any group of words that introduces a column, even if that group of words is not an independent clause. Capitalize the first letter of each entry in the list. (These two rules *are* standard.)

5:05 When the information in the column is made up of items, people's names, or phrases and are not independent clauses, do not place periods after the entries.

At the business session, Elmer Stewart received:
   A five-year service medal
   Two letters of commendation
   A promotion from communications supervisor to district manager

The following employees will be transferred to Denver:
   •Wanda Curry
   •Raymond Harris
   •Kawanna McClain

Juanita Pinder will explain the procedures for:
   A. Submitting budget requests
   B. Tracking expense accounts
   C. Applying for transfers and promotions

5:06 When the information in the column is made up of independent clauses, place the appropriate punctuation mark after each entry.

Before we sign the lease:
   1. The carpets must be replaced.
   2. The walls must be painted.
   3. All appliances in the cafeteria must be checked to make sure they work properly.

By tomorrow afternoon, we should be able to answer the following questions:
   Are any of the employees willing to take early retirement?
   Is our cash flow likely to improve over the next six months?
   Should we invest more or less in the bond market?

5:07 NOTE: Logic (parallelism) requires that each item in a list follow the form set by the first item. If the first item in that list is a name, all of the items must be names. If the first item is a phrase, all of the items must be phrases. If the first item is a sentence, all of the items must be sentences. If the first item is a question, all of the items must be questions.

DASHES

5:08 Dashes are commonly used in informal messages to represent pauses or shifts in thought. They seldom find a place in business writing. Only one situation calls for a dash as a normal punctuation mark in business correspondence.

5:09 Use a dash when a list precedes an independent clause.

Ambition, hard work, and honesty—<u>these traits sent him to an early grave</u>.

5:10 CAUTION: Do not use this dash unless an independent clause follows it. The following sentence uses a dash incorrectly:

Ambition, hard work, and honesty—are the traits that sent him to an early grave.

To correct this sentence, drop the dash.

Ambition, hard work, and honesty are the traits that sent him to an early grave.

5:11 **EXERCISE 5**
COLONS AND DASHES

Add the missing colons, dashes, and periods.
1. They furnished all of the wood the logs, the beams, and the studs.
2. The company will pay most of your expenses for example, food, travel, and lodging.
3. Cathy Gomez, Sally Berk, and Alice Jenkins each of these employees deserves our deep appreciation.
4. With your claim, please submit the following documentation
    Your preapproved authorization to travel
    Your meal receipts
    Your mileage records

5. With your claim, please submit your
    •Travel voucher
    •Meal receipts
    •Mileage records

6. When you turn in your claim, please
    A. Submit your travel log
    B. Turn in your expense records
    C. Sign the travel voucher

7. Blue, green, red, and brown are her favorite colors.
8. Don't forget to bring the eating utensils the knives, the forks, and the spoons.
9. Typing, taking dictation, and answering the phone those tasks occupy most of an administrative assistant's day.
10. During the break, we served coffee, fruit juice, and doughnuts.
11. She has several assets namely, intelligence, perseverance, and an understanding manner.

6 CAPITALIZATION

6:01 Few people approach capitalization confidently. As a result, most writers capitalize far too many words. The five rules in this chapter will help you avoid the common errors.

1. PERSONAL TITLES AND POSITIONS

6:02 Capitalize all titles that immediately precede a person's name.

Ask Aunt Pat to see President Jones about the books for Mayor Klein and Sheriff Davis.

When a title does not immediately precede a person's name, *DO NOT* capitalize the title unless it satisfies *both* of the following requirements:

6:03 1. It *must* be a high-level position of public trust (lieutenant governor and above in the US as well as important officials in foreign governments and international organizations).
AND

6:04 2. You *must* have a specific individual in mind. If you could use a person's name in place of the title (without changing the sentence structure), capitalize it.

The mayor of San Francisco wants to become a United States senator, but first she wants to serve as the ambassador to Thailand.

We could substitute a person's name for *mayor*, but it is below lieutenant governor. We can't substitute a person's name for a United States *senator* or *ambassador*. For these reasons, none of them are capitalized.

The President (of the US) and the Governor (of California) met with England's Prime Minister and the Pope to work for the release of our Ambassador.

We could have named these "high-level, public-trust" individuals, but we used their titles in place of their names. We *must* capitalize them.

6:05 *Do not* capitalize the title of a private citizen unless it precedes the name.

My aunt will talk to the president (of a company) about working as a secretary II.

2. SHORTENED GEOGRAPHIC NAMES

6:06 Capitalize shortened geographic terms when they refer to a specific geographic region.

Bill is from the South, and Anne is from the Midwest, but they met on the West Coast.

3. NAMES OF COMPANIES, ORGANIZATIONS, AND DEPARTMENTS

6:07 Capitalize the names of companies and organizations just as you capitalize titles. (See 6:13.)

US Petroleum applied for a loan from The State Bank of Trade and Commerce.

6:08 Do not capitalize shortened versions of names like *our company* and *the bank*.

6:09 Do, however, capitalize widely used nicknames for specific organizations.

the Corps ⟼ the US Army Corps of Engineers or the US Marine Corps
the Hill ⟼ Capitol Hill
Georgia Tech ⟼ Georgia Institute of Technology

6:10 Capitalize the correct names of departments and divisions within an organization.

Tell our Accounting Department to work with our Shipping and Receiving Department to send these forms to their Accounting Department and to their people in Shipping and Receiving.

6:11 NOTE: Do not capitalize the term *federal* in such expressions as *federal government, federal agency,* and *federal regulations*.

4. BUILDINGS AND ROOMS
6:12 Capitalize the names of buildings and rooms.

We moved from ***Room 204*** in the ***L Building*** to ***Conference Room II*** in ***Warehouse C***.

5. TITLES, HEADINGS, AND MEMORANDUM SUBJECT LINES
6:13 Capitalize the first letters of all words in titles, headings, and subject lines except:

1. Articles (*a, an,* and *the*)
2. Coordinating conjunctions (*and, but, or, nor, yet* and, *so*)
3. Prepositions (*of, for, by, in, off, out, under, through,* etc)
    (*Gregg* capitalizes long prepositions like *under* and *through*. *Merriam-Webster* and *The Chicago Manual of Style* don't. *Gregg*'s approach is probably outdated.)

6:14 Capitalize even these articles, conjunctions, and prepositions when they are the first and last words of a title, a subtitle (following a colon or a dash), a heading, or a memorandum subject line.

6:15 Follow these rules even when hyphens combine words in titles (First-Class Travel).

6:16 We can avoid these complex rules by capitalizing every letter in a title, heading, or subject line.

6:17 NOTE: Titles of books, pamphlets, brochures, magazines, and newspapers are italicized. (Underline them if you are writing by hand or with a typewriter, which has no italics).Titles of magazine articles, newspaper articles, reports, and presentations are set in quotations marks. Software titles are simply capitalized (Super Chess, PhotoFix).

EXERCISE 6
CAPITALIZATION

6:18 I. Triple underline each lowercase letter that should be capitalized, and draw a slash through each capitalized letter that should be lowercase.

1. The Marshall County chamber of commerce sponsored the Fair.
2. His math professor grew up in western Ohio and spent his entire life in the north.
3. The Federal Government approved our corporation's health plan, but a house subcommittee is investigating the company that administers it.
4. When did chief justice Warren retire?
5. My Mother wrote uncle Bill and asked him to join our volunteer fire department.
6. Several Congresswomen from the sunbelt oppose senator Oak's proposal for federal aid to colleges and universities.
7. The vice president of the United States toured their personnel division.
8. The Head of our finance department resigned to take a job in Alabama on the gulf.
9. He applied for the position of computer programmer.

6:19 II. In the following titles, circle the letters that should be capitalized.

cutting the water off

a trip up and back down the Dow Jones average

open communications: a study of self-esteem

7 NUMBERS

7:01 When should numbers be written as numerals, and when should they be spelled? Literary, academic, and highly formal writers prefer to spell numbers while technical and scientific writers tend to use more numerals. Business writers take the middle ground. The six guidelines in this chapter apply to business writing.

1. NUMERALS OR SPELLED NUMBERS?

7:02 Under ordinary circumstances, spell the numbers zero through ten. Above ten, use numerals. This guideline applies to exact numbers (six, 17, 1901) and to approximations (at least five, around 15, almost 2,000).

Only *three* days ago, *27* of our volunteers took pledges from about *1500* callers.

7:03 *Exception 1*: When a single piece of writing would use both numerals and spelled numbers to refer to similar bits of information, use numerals for all of them.

All *14* employees agreed to meet with *3* members of the management team.

That car will go from *0* to *45* in only a few seconds.

7:04 If the numbers go with different types of things, we can use spelled numbers and numerals in the same piece of writing.

Within *two* weeks, *14* employees signed up for all *three* training sessions.

7:05 *Exception 2*: Spell *million*, *billion,* and *trillion* instead of using long rows of zeros.

Write *3,561,923,491*, but change *3,500,000,000* to *3.5 billion* (not 3.5 billions).

7:06 *Exception 3*: When a number that would normally be written as a numeral falls at the beginning of a sentence, spell it.

Twelve applicants had submitted their résumés by the end of the week.

Consider rearranging the sentence so you can use a numeral.

By the end of the week, *12* applicants had submitted their résumés.

7:07 *Exception 4*: Always use numerals with the word *percent*.

The new regulations affect *5 percent* of our employees and *12 percent* of our retirees.

7:08 *Exception 5*: Spell vague references to numbers (***hundreds, a few thousand, several million***). Words like ***about***, ***almost***, ***around***, ***more than***, ***over***, and ***under*** signal approximations, not vague references.

Over *350* (an approximation) people showed up, and we handed out *hundreds* (a vague reference) of pamphlets.

2. FRACTIONS

7:09 Spell fractions if they stand alone and involve only two words.

>*one-third* of our employees

7:10 Use numerals for fractions involving more than two words, for combinations of fractions and whole numbers, and for numbers with decimals.

>*1/64* of an inch, *5½* hours, *2.4* tons

7:11 Decimal numbers are easier to read than fractions that are combined with whole numbers.

>*5¼* liters ⟼ *5.25* liters

3. DATES

7:12 In a report or in the body of a letter, memorandum, or e-mail, you may use *the 1st of* (or *the first of*), *the 2d of* (or *the second of*), *the 3d of* (or *the third of*), and so on before the month, but use these expressions *only when the year is NOT mentioned*.

>He came on the *5th* (or *fifth*) of May and left on the *24th* (or *twenty-fourth*).

7:13 With or without the year, use only the numeral (no *th*, *st*, or *d*) after the month.

>He arrived on *May 5, 1990*, and left on *May 24*.

7:14 Many Americans now use the international format for dates.

>He arrived on *5 May 1990* and left on *24 May*.

Use one format or the other within a single piece of writing.

7:15 NOTE: Use diagonals with dates (*6/11/92*) only on forms where space is limited. Consider avoiding all dates with diagonals. As more people use the international format, dates like *6/11/92* could be read as *June 11, 1992*, or *6 November 1992*.

4. TIME

7:16 To write clock time, use numerals plus *AM* or *PM*. Use *12 midnight* and *12 noon* instead of *12 AM* and *12 PM* (but use *12:15 AM* and *12:35 PM*).

>Our plane will leave Seattle at *7:45 AM* and will land in New Orleans at *12 noon*.

7:17 NOTE: Some careful writers believe *12 noon* and *12 midnight* are redundancies. (See 18:32.) They believe *noon* and *midnight* can stand alone. Others think *noon* and *midnight* sound vague (like *morning, afternoon*, and *evening*) and choose the precision of *12 noon* and *12 midnight*. Either approach will cause less confusion than *12 AM* and *12 PM.*

7:18 Do not add *:00* unless you need the zeros to fill out the spaces in a column.

>| Arrivals | Departures |
>|---|---|
>| 2:15 AM | 2:45 AM |
>| 3*:00* PM | 3:30 PM |
>| 4:15 PM | 5*:00* PM |

English for Professionals 33

5. MONEY

7:19 Use the dollar symbol and numerals to write exact and approximate amounts of money.

The paper costs only *$3.95*, but the ink cartridge costs about *$15.*

7:20 Spell *million*, *billion*, and *trillion* instead of using long rows of zeros.

Last year's sales tax revenues exceeded *$3 million* (not $3 million<u>s</u>).

7:21 Do not add *.00* unless you need the zeros to fill out the spaces in a column.

$111.50
114.75
<u>20.*00*</u>
$246.25

7:22 Spell vague references to dollar amounts. (See 7:08.)
We invested thousands of dollars in that patent.

7:23 Use the word *cents* (not the ¢ symbol) or the dollar symbol for amounts less than a dollar. If you use the dollar symbol for amounts less than a dollar, do not put a zero in front of the decimal point. (The dollar symbol [*$*] and other monetary symbols, like those that represent the yen [¥] and the euro [€], are the only symbols commonly used in business writing. The ¢ symbol is not used.)

The gum is *5 cents* (or *$.05*), and the toy costs *65 cents* (or *$.65*).

7:24 When an amount of less than one dollar appears in the same piece of writing with an amount of one dollar or higher, always use the dollar symbol instead of the word *cents*. Do not put a zero in front of the decimal point.

The bat costs *$4.95*, but the ball is only *$.79*.

6. COMMAS AND DECIMAL POINTS

7:25 Use commas in numerals with more than three digits. Do not, however, use commas with the year of a date, and do not use commas in street addresses or ZIP codes.

We spent *$9,200* on *13,265* light bulbs for the offices at *2640* Broadway back in *2001*.

7:26 When you write decimal numerals (other than dollar amounts) smaller than one, put a zero in front of the decimal point. Do not use commas to the right of a decimal point.

0.25 acre
0.04278 parts per million
6.405283 centimeters

With dollar amounts, the dollar symbol replaces the zero. (See 7:24.)

$.59

7. PLURALS OF NUMBERS

7:27 To make a number plural, simply add *s*. Several years ago, *'s* was required, but the apostrophe has now been dropped.

They think the *'60s* and the *'90s* have much in common. (The apostrophe represents the missing *19*.)

EXERCISE 7
NUMBERS

I. Correct the errors in the following sentences.

1. On January 30th, they decided to sell all 5 computers for about thirteen thousand dollars.

2. She called at 12:00 PM and came over around 3:00 PM.

3. The report indicates that ¼ of their employees earn more than $20.00 an hour.

4. The pens cost $0.65 each, and the pads cost $1.25 each.

5. The car costs $22000 new, but a two-year-old model sells for about $8000.

6. The sausages average about .55 pounds each.

7. Place the order after 3 March but before April the 4th.

8. 19 people at the meeting invested several $1,000s in the project.

9. In eighteen hundred and three, Robert Livingston bought 530,000,000 acres for a little over $27,000,000.

10. Americans like to brag that Livingston paid only 3¢ an acre for the Louisiana Purchase, but the actual price was about 5¢ an acre.

11. Carlos Lopez, aged forty-two, is in charge of all 3 divisions.

12. By noon yesterday, seven doctors and 12 nurses had volunteered.

13. The state's budget deficit exceeded two and one-quarter billions of dollars.

14. In eighteen eighty-two, on 22 September, his great-grandmother was born in Norway.

15. 100s of our investors earned 1000s of dollars in the '70's.

II. Correct the errors in this paragraph.

Printing the brochures cost a few $100s more at PrintCo, but they delivered them by 12:00 PM on August 18th, and we had them in the mail fourteen days early. We sent out around twelve thousand brochures, and they generated fifteen thousand nine hundred and forty-five dollars in profit.

8 *WHO* OR *WHOM* *WHOEVER* OR *WHOMEVER*

8:01 Ordinarily, only serious students of traditional grammar understand the difference between *who* and *whom* As a result, *whom* is disappearing from our language and now sounds unnatural to the average American.

If you are determined to master the fine points of usage, study this chapter. After you examine the four cases discussed here, you should be able to use *whom* and *whomever* correctly.

CASE ONE: *WHO* OR *WHOM* USED IN A QUESTION WITH A PREPOSITION

8:02 The easiest *who*-or-*whom* decision comes with questions where *who* or *whom* follows a preposition.

To (or *For* or *About*) *whom* did she write the story?

Whom is always the correct choice in such cases.

PRACTICE 8-A
Choose between *who* and *whom*.
1. With **(who, whom)** will they travel to Juneau?
2. At **(who, whom)** did he aim the pistol?
3. From **(who, whom)** have we received responses?
4. For **(who, whom)** will he vote?
5. Near **(who, whom)** was she sitting?

8:03 Most of us recognize that all five sentences call for *whom*. Unfortunately, we seldom build sentences using this pattern. In modern usage, the preposition commonly (and correctly) falls at the end of the sentence. (See 18:12.)

(Who, Whom) did she address the letter to?
(Who, Whom) was the building designed for?

As far as the grammar is concerned, the situation is unchanged. The preposition still forces us to select *whom*, but many people mistakenly select *who*.

PRACTICE 8-B
Choose between *who* and *whom*. In the first five sentences, the prepositions have been underlined for you. In the final five, you must find them on your own.
1. **(Who, Whom)** did she depend <u>on</u> for support?
2. **(Who, Whom)** was he speaking <u>for</u> at the rally?
3. **(Who, Whom)** is the woman in the red dress <u>with</u>?
4. **(Who, Whom)** will the story be written <u>about</u>?
5. **(Who, Whom)** have we received orders <u>from</u>?
6. **(Who, Whom)** was the report written by?
7. **(Who, Whom)** did she mail the pamphlet to?
8. **(Who, Whom)** should we buy the parts from?
9. **(Who, Whom)** were they camping with?
10. **(Who, Whom)** will they be living near?

CASE TWO: WHO OR WHOM IN A QUESTION WITHOUT A PREPOSITION

8:04   A more complicated *who*-or-*whom* decision comes in questions where the *who* or the *whom* has nothing to do with a preposition.

>   **(Who, Whom)** wrote the report?
>
>   **(Who, Whom)** did Robert hire?

In the first example, *who* is correct. In the second, it's *whom*. Why?

The following two statements explain the use of every *who, whom, whoever,* and *whomever* you will ever see or hear.

1. Use *who* when you could replace it with *he, she,* or *they*. Think "*He, she,* or *they* calls for *who*."

   Who (not *whom*) wrote the report?

   He (or *she* or *they*) wrote the report.

2. Use *whom* when you could replace it with *him, her,* or *them*. Think "*Him, her,* or *them* calls for *whom*."

   Whom (not *who*) did Robert hire?

   Robert hired *him* (or *her* or *them*).

PRACTICE 8-C
Choose between *who* and *whom*.

1. **(Who, Whom)** must he defeat to become champion?
2. **(Who, Whom)** was your opponent in the final match?
3. **(Who, Whom)** will you pick up on your way to work?
4. **(Who, Whom)** started the move to increase profits?
5. **(Who, Whom)** will you be meeting at the conference?
6. **(Who, Whom)** was her best friend in college?
7. **(Who, Whom)** will we take to the club tonight?
8. **(Who, Whom)** carried out the board's orders?
9. **(Who, Whom)** did they elect to serve as chairperson?
10. **(Who, Whom)** asked for the assignment first?

Look back over PRACTICE 8-B and PRACTICE 8-C. Notice that none of the *whom*s can be dropped without destroying the meaning of the sentences. (Notice also that all of these sentences are questions that ask for a person's name.)

The importance of these observations will be clear when you do EXERCISE 8-B, "Avoiding *Whom* and *Whomever*," on page 42.

English for Professionals 37

CASE THREE: WHO OR WHOM STARTING A DEPENDENT CLAUSE

8:05 Deciding between *who* and *whom* is slightly more difficult when the *who* or *whom* is the first word of a dependent clause.

What is a *dependent clause*? The word *clause* refers to a group of words with a subject and a verb. An *independent clause* has a subject and a verb and can stand alone as a sentence. A *dependent clause* has a subject and a verb but can't stand alone as a sentence. Dependent clauses are easier to spot than they are to explain.

The following example illustrates how *who* can open a dependent clause:

   Mr. Jones is the one *who* brought the cheesecake.

The dependent clause, *who* brought the cheesecake, has a subject (who) and a verb (brought), but it can't stand alone.

In the next example, *whom* opens the dependent clause:

   Ms. Wilson is the one *whom* Mr. Jones brought to the reception.

The dependent clause, *whom* Mr. Jones brought to the reception, has a subject (Mr. Jones) and a verb (brought), but it can't stand alone.

Why is **who** correct in one example while *whom* is correct in another? Convert the dependent clauses into independent clauses, and the answer will be obvious.

In the first example, convert who brought the cheesecake to "*He* (*she* or *they*) brought the cheesecake." *Who* is the correct choice. (Remember, *he, she,* or *they* calls for *who*.)

In the second, convert *whom* Mr. Jones brought to the reception to "Mr. Jones brought *her* (*him* or *them*) to the reception." *Whom* is the correct choice. (Remember, *him, her,* or *them* calls for *whom*.)

PRACTICE 8-D
Choose between *who* and *whom*. The dependent clauses have been underlined for you in the first five sentences. For sentences 6 through 15, you should underline the dependent clauses. Convert all of the dependent clauses to independent clauses before you choose between *who* and *whom*.

1. She interviewed the driver **(who, whom)** took first place at Daytona.
2. The woman **(who, whom)** we promoted is his sister.
3. Karl and Kit, the boys **(who, whom)** you read the book to, are five years old.
4. The one **(who, whom)** finishes last will win the contest.
5. The little girl **(who, whom)** you saw on TV is a gifted actress.
6. The one **(who, whom)** drove the car wasn't even hurt.
7. The elderly man **(who, whom)** was honored at the banquet is our founder.
8. We know two people **(who, whom)** moved to Australia.
9. The ladies **(who, whom)** you investigated are here.
10. We hired the one **(who, whom)** had the neatest résumé.
11. She sends contributions to the artists **(who, whom)** she believes are deserving.

12. The doctor **(who, whom)** they prefer is a graduate of Central Medical School.

13. Ms. Foster, the woman **(who, whom)** they gave the records to, is incredibly fast.

14. Everyone **(who, whom)** achieved the goal will earn an extra day of vacation.

15. Did they say **(who, whom)** it was? (See the NOTE ON SENTENCE 15 [8:06-07].)

Whom sounds stilted to the average American. Can any of these *whom*s be dropped? If so, mark them out. Do the sentences sound more natural now?

8:06 NOTE ON SENTENCE 15: Did you incorrectly circle *whom* in sentence 15? If you did, you probably thought to yourself, "It was *him*, it was *her*, it was *them*."

Those phrases might sound correct, but according to the logic of grammar, they are incorrect. You should have thought, "It was *he*, it was *she*, it was *they*." Why?

According to the logic of grammar, when a pronoun follows the verb *to be* (we use the verb *to be* in the forms *am, are, is, was, were, will be, have been,* etc), the pronoun must be in the nominative case (*I, you, he, she, they,* and *we*). According to the logic of grammar, the following awkward expressions are correct:

That boy on the left is *I* (while looking at a photograph).

That should be *they* now (after hearing a knock on the door).

This is *she* (when answering the telephone).

If these expressions follow the logic of grammar, why do they sound awkward? Are we speaking poor English when we say "That should be *them* now"?

Some good writers say **YES** and believe we should retrain our ears to accept "That boy on the left is *I*." In fact, many administrative assistants are now trained to say "This is *she*" when answering the telephone.

On the other hand, linguists tell us that these expressions, though they don't obey the laws of traditional grammar, are actually long-respected idioms that the French-speaking Normans brought to England in the year 1066. (Idioms are illogical expressions that the linguistic community accepts as correct, and our language has countless idioms.) In French, the expressions "That is *me*," "That is *him*," and "That is *them*" are perfectly correct.

When we look at a picture and say, "That boy on the left is *me*," we are using the long-respected idiom. When we say "That boy on the left is I," we are following the logic of grammar (and are probably guilty of pomposity). In most cases, the choice is ours, but when we choose between *who* and *whom*, we must rely on the logic of grammar: it was *he*, it was *she*, it was *they*.

8:07 Whenever the *who*-or-*whom* decision is tied to some form of the verb *to be*, we always select *who*.

PRACTICE 8-E
Choose between who and whom.

1. When I tell you **(who, whom)** they <u>are</u>, you will be shocked.

2. He already knows **(who, whom)** the new president <u>will be</u>.

3. **(Who, Whom)** <u>was</u> she <u>looking</u> for?

4. We simply have no idea **(who, whom)** the embezzler <u>might have been</u>.

5. If he would tell us **(who, whom)** the executor <u>is</u>, we could pay you now.

English for Professionals

CASE FOUR: WHOEVER OR WHOMEVER

8:08 CASE FOUR deals with the choice between *whoever* and *whomever*. If you understand CASE THREE, choosing between *whoever* and *whomever* will be easy.

(Whoever, Whomever) wins the race will be rich.
(Whoever, Whomever) we name acting president must agree to take risks.
Give the film to **(whoever, whomever)** comes to the meeting wearing a red scarf.

In the first example, convert **(whoever, whomever)** wins the race to an independent clause. "*He* (or *she* or *they*) wins the race." *Whoever* is correct because *he*, *she*, or *they* calls for *who*.

In the second example, convert **(whoever, whomever)** we name to "We name *him* (or *her* or *them*)." *Whomever* is correct because *him*, *her*, or *them* calls for *whom*.

In the third, *whoever* is correct. Many people, even good writers, would mistakenly select *whomever* because they concentrate on the words "to **(whoever, whomever)**" and think "To *him*, to *her*, or to *them* calls for *whom*," but the *to* is not part of the dependent clause.

8:09 CAUTION: *Consider only the words within the dependent clause* when you choose between *whoever* and *whomever*.

Give the film to *whoever* comes to the meeting wearing a red scarf.

Whoever comes to the meeting is correct because "*He* (or *she* or *they*) comes to the meeting," and *he*, *she*, or *they* calls for *who*. Here is another example:

Give the film to **(whoever, whomever)** we meet on the bus.

Convert **(whoever, whomever)** we meet on the bus to "We meet *him* (or *her* or *them*) on the bus." This time *whomever* is correct (*him*, *her* or *them* calls for *whom*), but the answer still has nothing to do with the word *to*.

PRACTICE 8-F
Choose between *whoever* and *whomever*. The dependent clauses have been underlined for you in the first five sentences. For sentences 6 through 10, you should underline the dependent clauses. Convert all of the dependent clauses to independent clauses before you choose the correct word.

1. Ask **(whoever, whomever)** you want for help with the drawings.
2. **(Whoever, Whomever)** you invite will be all right with us.
3. **(Whoever, Whomever)** angers her will be in serious trouble.
4. She behaves courteously toward **(whoever, whomever)** works in her division.
5. He will try to defeat **(whoever, whomever)** he thinks is corrupt.
6. We must hire **(whoever, whomever)** we can find with the proper credentials.
7. Tell her to ride with **(whoever, whomever)** lives in her area.
8. **(Whoever, Whomever)** we ask to speak must possess a healthy sense of humor.
9. Buy your supplies from **(whoever, whomever)** she has an account with.
10. Ask **(whoever, whomever)** is on the phone to call later.

Whomever sounds stilted to the average American ear. Substitute *anyone whom* or *the person whom* for *whomever*. Can any of the *whoms* now be dropped? Do the sentences sound more natural?

EXERCISE 8a
WHO OR *WHOM*, *WHOEVER* OR *WHOMEVER*

Circle the correct word. If the word in question starts a dependent clause, underline the dependent clause, convert it to an independent clause, and then choose the correct word.

1. **(Who, Whom)** is the best choice for mayor?

2. **(Who, Whom)** has she been talking to?

3. The job will go to the person **(who, whom)** writes the fastest.

4. We made sure plenty of paper was available to **(whoever, whomever)** needed it.

5. If you know **(who, whom)** the suspect is, don't say a word.

6. She is the only representative **(who, whom)** we will be sending to California.

7. He left those keys for the people **(who, whom)** work in the computer center.

8. He accepts support from **(whoever, whomever)** is willing to back him.

9. He doesn't believe the program will appeal to the customer **(who, whom)** it was designed for.

10. They have posted the names of the students **(who, whom)** the director chose for the parts.

11. We believe that we can predict **(who, whom)** the winner will be.

12. From **(who, whom)** did you buy your car?

13. Extensive training is needed for **(whoever, whomever)** works with the word processor.

14. I reviewed the résumés of the applicants **(who, whom)** she thought were qualified.

15. The associate **(who, whom)** accumulated the most overtime earned the largest raise.

16. We will cooperate with **(whoever, whomever)** they send to work with us.

17. **(Who, Whom)** will they leave their children with?

18. The agency hired Clara Foy, the woman **(who, whom)** worked for you last summer.

19. She will accept **(whoever, whomever)** we send.

20. The used furniture was given to the man **(who, whom)** Ms. Jenkins had helped before.

21. **(Whoever, Whomever)** the best candidate might have been, we decided to hire Sharon.

22. We answer to **(whoever, whomever)** is in charge of production.

23. When you were in Maine, **(who, whom)** did you work under?

24. **(Who, Whom)** did you bury in the basement?

English for Professionals   41

25. **(Who, Whom)** are the people primarily responsible for the audits?

26. **(Whoever, Whomever)** you pick will be sent to Alaska.

27. **(Whoever, Whomever)** attended the party can't be considered a suspect.

28. **(Who, Whom)** did she interview this morning?

29. The child **(who, whom)** won the contest is my niece.

30. He gives the information to **(whoever, whomever)** he assumes will back us.

31. Give the package to **(whoever, whomever)** is willing to sign the receipt.

32. They called in to ask **(who, whom)** was appointed to fill Joe's seat.

33. From **(who, whom)** did you order the parts?

34. Did she ask **(who, whom)** it was **(who, whom)** wrote the letter?

35. We will hire **(whoever, whomever)** they recommend.

After you have checked your answers, go back over this exercise, and examine each correct *whom*. If you find one you can drop, mark it out. Do the sentences sound more natural now?

Do any of the *whom*s refuse to be dropped? Why?

Now examine each correct *whomever*. Change them to *anyone*, *the person*, or some similar phrase. Do the sentences sound more natural now?

Do any of the *whomever*s refuse to be changed to *anyone* or *the person*?

CLOSING COMMENTS
If you studied this chapter carefully, you know how to use *who, whom, whoever,* and *whomever* correctly. Here are three more things you have probably learned.

8:11
- *Whom* causes so much trouble and sounds stilted because we seldom use it. We usually drop it from our sentences (CASE THREE).

8:12
- The same is true of *whomever*. We usually replace it with *anyone, the person*, or some similar phrase (CASE FOUR).

8:13
- *Whom* is often difficult or impossible to avoid when we ask questions, especially when the answer calls for someone's name (CASE ONE and CASE TWO). In these instances, we need to know the difference between who and *whom.*

8:14 **EXERCISE 8b**
AVOIDING WHOM AND WHOMEVER

Many people think the words *whom* and *whomever* sound stilted. Using standard English, alter the following sentences to avoid *whom* and *whomever* wherever possible.

You can drop some of the *whom*s and change the *whomever*s to *anyone*, *the person*, or some similar phrase, but a few of the *whom*s will be unavoidable.

1. He will vote for whomever she nominates.

2. He is one of the children to whom we wrote letters.

3. Whom did he address when he spoke?

4. Has she seen the man whom they asked her to hire?

5. The young woman will have to marry whomever her father selects.

6. From whom did you receive the telegram?

7. He sent us the names of three men whom he will accept.

8. Whomever they send will be able to handle the job.

9. Sara Clark, the woman whom you met last week, will be your supervisor.

10. Whom did you talk to?

11. That man is the one whom I introduced to you this morning.

12. Whom can we depend on to clear up the misunderstanding?

13. We send free samples to whomever she puts on the list.

14. Did you see the children whom she brought on the tour?

15. Whomever they select as judge must be fully qualified.

9 ABBREVIATIONS

9:01 Abbreviations are a type of shorthand. Don't overuse them. Good writers are most likely to use abbreviations when space is at a premium (when filling out forms, for example) or when the message is informal and the reader will easily understand the abbreviations.

These eight guidelines will help you use abbreviations correctly when you write for business.

1. IN HIGHLY FORMAL DOCUMENTS

9:02 Keep abbreviations to an absolute minimum in highly formal documents like résumés and exceptionally important letters.

2. IN ROUTINE LETTERS, MEMORANDUMS, AND E-MAILS

9:03 In routine letters, memorandums, and e-mails, do not use abbreviations unless they are pronounced the way they are written. For example, use *TVA*, *IBM*, or *Btu*, but don't use *TX* (except in addresses), *Mon*, or *corp*. (Almost all of our spoken abbreviations are acronyms.)

9:04 *Exceptions*: Use the following abbreviations only when they precede or follow a person's name: *Ms., Mrs., Mr., Dr, Jr,* and *Sr,* and *Esq.* Also, *et cetera* is also commonly written as *etc*. Use *Corp* and *Inc* with company names if the companies themselves abbreviate those words.

9:05 NOTE: The comma between a person's name and *Sr, Jr, III,* or *Esq* is no longer required, nor is the comma between a company's name and *Inc*. (*Esq* is used with both male and female lawyers.)

3. WEIGHTS AND MEASURES

9:06 In routine letters, memorandums, and e-mails, do not abbreviate the units used for weights and measures (use *pound* instead of *lb*, *foot* instead of *ft,* and *centimeter* instead of *cm*).

4. SYMBOLS

9:07 In routine letters, memorandums, and e-mails, avoid symbols (*@, &, #, %,* etc). Instead, spell the words they represent. These symbols are for tables and forms where space is limited.

Exception: When you deal with specific or approximate amounts of money, use *$* or another monetary symbol, like ¥ or €, and express the amount in numerals. (See 7:19-24.)

5. DEFINING AND CREATING ABBREVIATIONS

9:08 If your reader might not be familiar with an abbreviation, give the full phrase, and follow it with the abbreviation in parentheses, or if you prefer, give the abbreviation, and follow it with the full phrase in parentheses. Once you have defined the abbreviation, you may use it freely.

Tennessee Valley Authority (TVA) *or* TVA (Tennessee Valley Authority)

You can use this method to create your own abbreviations.

personnel efficiency training (PET) project *or* PET (personnel efficiency training) project

6. PLURALS OF ABBREVIATIONS

9:09 To form the plural of an abbreviation, simply add a lowercase *s* (*Btus, RNs, YMCAs*).

Exception: If the abbreviation ends with a lowercase letter *and* a period follows it, add *'s* (*i.e.'s, Mr.'s*).

7. POSSESSIVES OF ABBREVIATIONS

9:10 To form the possessive of an abbreviation, add *'s* (*CEO's, RN's, USA's,* etc).

8. ABBREVIATIONS AND PERIODS

9:11 Does an abbreviation require you to add periods? The answer depends largely on which handbook or dictionary you consult. One dictionary lists *FDIC* but another gives *F.D.I.C.* One handbook calls for *Ms.* while another prefers *Ms* (without the period).

In 1990, *Merriam-Webster* stripped the periods from all abbreviations except *e.g., i.e., Ms., Mrs.,* and *Mr.* The initials used with people's names (Louis *C.* Chung) also take periods. When *Corp* and *Inc* appear in a company name, add the period if the company itself adds the period.

This book, *CommonSense Grammar and Style*, leaves periods off abbreviations wherever *Merriam-Webster* leaves them off, but many respected authorities, including *Gregg*, still add the periods.

9:12 **EXERCISE 9**
ABBREVIATIONS

I. Correct the abbreviation errors.

1. William R. Cook Junior will be our new co. pres.
2. They had to hire two C.P.A.'s to take her place.
3. When he hit the ice, he locked the brakes and slid about 100 ft..
4. American Mining Corp. is one of the most prosperous corps. in our area.
5. She served three years as a CPO (chief petty officer) in the United States Navy.
6. About 60% of the employees will attend the party, and the # one attraction will be Mr Williams' magic show.
7. She ordered four of them @ 5 dollars each.
8. Our daughter is a Jr in high school.
9. He must have taken his management courses around 1000 bc.
10. Their CEOs computer is being repaired.

9:13 II. Treat the following paragraph as though a US Army officer wrote it for people interested in visiting a specific military base.

The SBOPs require citizens of the USA and Canada to obtain written permission from the com. off. before entering the base. Officials of the KY and TN gov.'s need only sign in at the gate. Sun.'s thru Fri.'s, all civ. visitors must be off base by 11 P.M.

10 COMPARATIVES AND SUPERLATIVES

10:01 *Comparatives* and *superlatives* are words like *bigger* and *biggest*. Comparatives, like *bigger*, compare two things, and superlatives, like *biggest*, compare three or more things. *Comparatives* and *superlatives* seldom cause trouble, but you might want to review them. Pay close attention to Sections 10:06 and 10:10. They treat the areas where most mistakes are made.

1. ONE-SYLLABLE WORDS

10:02 One-syllable adjectives add *-er* to form the comparative and *-est* to form the superlative.

    fast   faster   fastest
    nice   nicer   nicest

2. TWO-SYLLABLE WORDS

10:03 Most two-syllable adjectives can use either *-er* and *-est* or *more* and *most*.

    hardy   hardier   hardiest
    or
    hardy   more hardy   most hardy

Although some two-syllable words (like *little, littler,* and *littlest*) always use *-er* and *-est*, the general tendency with two-syllable adjectives is to use *more* and *most*.

3. WORDS WITH THREE OR MORE SYLLABLES

10:04 Adjectives with three or more syllables use *more* for the comparative and *most* for the superlative.

    incredible   more incredible   most incredible
    disastrous   more disastrous   most disastrous

10:05 Exception 1: Two-syllable adjectives ending with common suffixes (*-less, -ous, -ful, -ing,* etc) must use *more* and *most*.

    nervous   more nervous   most nervous
    mindless   more mindless   most mindless
    peaceful   more peaceful   most peaceful

10:06 Exception 2: All adverbs that end with *-ly* use *more* and *most*. Never throw away the *-ly* to form the comparative or the superlative.

    warmly   more warmly (not warmer)   most warmly (not warmest)
    lightly   more lightly (not lighter)   most lightly (not lightest)

10:07 Exception 3: Some words form irregular comparatives and superlatives.

    good   better   best
    many   more   most
    bad   worse   worst

10:08 *Exception 4*: With some words (*dead, perfect, round, unique,* etc), comparatives and superlatives are not logically possible. Use phrases like *nearly perfect, more nearly perfect,* and *most nearly perfect*.

4. DOUBLING COMPARATIVE AND SUPERLATIVE FORMS

10:09 Never combine the comparative form of a word with *more*. Never combine the superlative form of a word with *most*.

    more stupider (incorrect)
    most craziest (incorrect)

5. THE SUPERLATIVE FORM WITH TWO ITEMS

10:10 Never use the superlative form when you compare only two people or things.

    Sharon is the tallest of our two centers. (incorrect)
    Sharon is the taller of our two centers. (correct)

10:11 **EXERCISE 10a**
COMPARATIVES AND SUPERLATIVES
Fill in the blanks. First, add the comparative of the italicized word. Next, add the superlative. Where comparative and superlative degrees are not logically possible, use *more nearly* and *most nearly*.

1. Scott is *short*, but Kent is _____ than Scott, and Pearl is the _____ of the three.

2. Her solo was *wonderful*, but Ted's solo was _____ than hers, and Dan's solo was the _____ we heard all day.

3. Our kitten is *playful*, but their kitten is _____ than ours, and Leon's kitten is the _____ I have ever seen.

4. *Much* of the work was done on Monday, and _____ of it was done on Tuesday, but _____ of it was done on Saturday when all of us were there.

5. Our pool is *shallow*, but her pool is _____, and the neighbor's pool is the _____ pool in town.

6. The first wall we put up is nearly *plumb*, but the second one is _____ than the first, and the one we just finished is the _____ of all.

7. Joy solved the problem *quickly*, and Ray solved it even _____. Still, Tomeka solved it _____.

10:12 **EXERCISE 10b**
COMPARATIVES AND SUPERLATIVES
Correct the following sentences.

1. Brian is the best of their two first team linebackers.

2. She's the most nicest person I know.

3. Tammy is more pregnant than Evelyn.

11 PLURALS

11:01 Since most nouns form their plurals by adding *s*, plurals cause few problems, but in five cases, plurals can be tricky. The guidelines in this chapter will help.

1. NOUNS THAT END WITH AN "S" SOUND

11:02 Most nouns that end with an "S" sound (*s, ch, sh, x,* or *z*) add *es* to form the plural.

    boss ⟼ bosses   brush ⟼ brushes
    church ⟼ churches   tax ⟼ taxes

11:03 An important exception can occur when people's names end with *s, ch, sh, x,* or *z*. Most of them follow the rule and form the plural by adding *es.*

    Mr. Busch ⟼ the Busches   Ms. Fox ⟼ the Foxes

11:04 If, however, adding the extra syllable makes the plural difficult to pronounce, use the singular form as the plural form.

    Ms. Bridges ⟼ the Bridges   Dr Moyers ⟼ the Moyers

11:05 NOTE: You might choose to add *es* where another person would leave the plural unchanged from the singular, and you would both be correct.

    Mr. Gates ⟼ the Gateses or the Gates

Remember, do not add *es* unless you add a syllable when you pronounce the plural.

PRACTICE 11-A

Fill in the blanks with the plurals of the italicized words.

1. If we buy this **box** and that **box**, we will have two _____.
2. Brad and Dot **Nash** are our friends. We play bridge with the _____.
3. Mr. **Huffines** brought his wife, and I believe the _____ had a good time.
4. This **gas** is colorless and that one isn't, but both _____ are inexpensive.
5. Gayle **Jacobs** and her children were there, and all of the _____ won a prize.

2. NOUNS THAT END WITH ST

11:06 Nouns that end with *st* add *s* to form the plural (request ⟼ requests), even though the final *s* is hard to pronounce.

3. NOUNS THAT END WITH O

11:07 If the *o* follows a vowel, add *s* to form the plural.

    zoo ⟼ zoos   folio ⟼ folios

11:08 If the *o* follows a consonant, the plural could add *s* or *es*. Consult a dictionary for the plurals of such words.

    potato ⟼ potatoes   placebo ⟼ placebos

4. NOUNS THAT END WITH Y

11:09   Most nouns that end with *y* form the plural by dropping the *y* and adding *ies* (berry ↦ berries).

11:10   If the *y* follows a vowel, the plural simply adds an *s* (boy ↦ boys, attorney ↦ attorneys).

5. NOUNS MADE OF TWO OR MORE WORDS

11:11   Compound nouns written as one word form their plurals by making the last word plural (bookkeeper ↦ bookkeepers, eyetooth ↦ eyeteeth).

11:12   When the compound noun is hyphenated or written as two or more words, it forms its plural by making the most important word plural (son-in-law ↦ sons-in-law, attorney general ↦ attorneys general).

PRACTICE 11-B
Fill in the blanks with the plurals of the italicized words.

1. I like the Irish *folksinger*, and she likes the one from England, but both _____ are talented.
2. He wore one *cast* on his arm and another on his leg, so he wore two _____.
3. There's a *quarry* in Kent and one in Burns, and both _____ sell high-quality stone.
4. Her *portfolio* earned 13 percent and his earned 11 percent, but both of their _____ are high-risk.
5. Our *chamber of commerce* competes with theirs, but both_____ are doing well.
6. His last *concerto* is my favorite, but all of his _____ are moving.
7. One *sister-in-law* is his supervisor and the other is his assistant. He enjoys working with both of his _____.
8. Their *attorney* met with ours and wrote a contract that both _____ think is fair.

IRREGULAR PLURALS

11:13   Many nouns form irregular plurals.

   goose ↦ geese   child ↦ children   tooth ↦ teeth

These common irregular plurals seldom cause trouble, but uncommon irregular plurals often confuse us.

   matrix ↦ matrices   criterion ↦ criteria   datum ↦ data

Almost everyone handles common irregular plurals correctly. One hallmark of careful writers is that they master the irregular plurals that are uncommon. When you discover a new irregular plural, memorize it.

English for Professionals　　49

11:14 **EXERCISE 11**
FORMING PLURALS
Fill in the blanks with the possessive forms of the italicized words.

1. I have one *cameo* and you have one *cameo*. Together, we have two _____.
2. Each county has an *attorney general*, and these _____ often consult with one another.
3. He owned one old *ox* and one young *ox*, but his _____ still worked well together.
4. One *Betsy Ross* lives on Main, another lives on Vine Street, and a third lives on First Avenue. Our town has three _____.
5. Each man owns a *steamship*, and their _____ are now docked in Boston.
6. One *buoy* marks the entrance to the marina, and the other marks the exit, but both _____ are painted red.
7. One *man-of-war* was French, and the other was British, and both _____ wanted to control access to the harbor.
8. One *tomato* was red and one was yellow but both _____ were delicious.
9. This *ax* is for chopping, and that one is for throwing. This week, both _____ are on sale.
10. They took one *X ray* of her arm and one of her foot. Both _____ should be back within an hour.
11. This *cactus* is native to Arizona, and that one is native to New Mexico, but both of the _____ are beautiful.
12. When they fell, Kai broke her left *wrist*, but Lloyd broke both of his _____.
13. Ms. *Summers* and her husband live in Seattle, and their children live in Cambridge. All of the _____ met in Colorado Springs for Thanksgiving.
14. Her *micro* is more advanced than his, but both _____ are fast enough to handle this program.
15. The first *jury* convicted her and the second *jury* acquitted her. Oddly enough, both _____ based their verdicts on the same evidence.
16. We have one *daughter-in-law* in Houston and another in Newark. Both _____ are physicians.
17. I had placed one *parenthesis* to the left of the word and one to the right, but both _____ faced the wrong direction.
18. Mr. *Baggins* inherited his parents' farm, and Ms. *Baggins* bought her brother's farm. Together, the _____ own over 1500 acres.
19. We shipped one *mast* to New England and the other to Florida. Both of the _____ were crafted from premium red spruce.
20. Mr. and Ms. *Stutz* have a new car, and the _____ will drive it to Mexico.

12 POSSESSIVES

12:01   Possessives appear to be simple, but they can cause massive confusion. Study this chapter carefully.

Possessives are usually formed with apostrophes. They allow us to avoid the word *of*, and they add great flexibility to the English language.

> The employees *of* our company are loyal.
> **or**
> Our company*'s* employees are loyal.

12:02   Many people confuse possessives with plurals. Most possessives use an apostrophe to establish a relationship between people or things (Jill's husband, her husband's car, the car's fender). Plurals simply stand for "more than one" (two husbands, eight cars, several fenders). Can you tell which words in the following passage are possessive and which are plural? Underline the possessive words, and circle the words that are simply plural.

> John's sisters are members of his church's choir, and his brothers all belong to the community's crime-prevention units. Nevertheless, John's best friends are all bums.

John's, church's, community's, and ***John's*** are possessive.
Sisters, members, brothers, units, friends, and ***bums*** are simply plural.

To use possessives correctly, you must learn two rules and four exceptions to the rules.

RULE ONE
12:03   If a word *does not* end with *s*, form the possessive by adding *'s* (the butcher's shop, the women's chairs).

12:04   ### RULE TWO
If a word *does* end with *s*, form the possessive by placing an apostrophe after the *s* (the two boys' pets, Mr. Parks' garden).

PRACTICE 12-A
Fill in the blanks with the possessive forms of the italicized words.

1. She lives on a *street* near two parks, and the _____ name is Walnut.
2. Both of my *brothers* paint, and my _____ paintings are selling well.
3. The *program* is here, but the _____ instructions are written in code.
4. All three *babies* are fine, but the _____ doctor is still running tests.
5. We talked with the *president*, and the _____ plans include all of us.
6. The *man* was here, but the _____ wife was downstairs.
7. Her *mother-in-law* is a lawyer, and her _____ offices are in New Jersey.
8. Our clinics employ thirty *nurses*, and the _____ schedules are flexible.
9. The *attorney general* met with him, and the _____ decisions will affect us all.
10. The *box* is in the safe, so the _____ contents are well-kept secrets.

Now go back, and circle the words that are simply plural.

When you want to make a word possessive, don't worry about whether the word is singular or plural. The question is, Does it end with *s*, or doesn't it?

PRACTICE 12-B

Fill in the blanks with the possessive forms of the italicized words.

1. They have three *children*, and the _____ playrooms are huge.

2. *Ms. Moyers* was promoted, and _____ salary was doubled.

3. The *chests of drawers* are cherry, and the _____ hardware is brass.

4. The *criteria* are clear but the _____ effectiveness is being questioned.

5. Our two *sons-in-law* are from Rio, but all four of our _____ parents are French.

Now go back, and circle the words that are simply plural.

12:05 **INDEFINITE PRONOUNS**

Anybody, anyone, everybody, everyone, nobody, no one, one, somebody, and *someone,* follow rule one. They form their possessives by adding *'s* (everybody's food, someone's umbrella).

PRACTICE 12-C

Fill in the blanks with the possessive forms of the italicized words.

1. *Everyone* is here, and _____ interests are well represented.

2. *No one* tried the pasta, so _____ opinions will be considered.

3. *Somebody* applied for the loans, so _____ assets will have to be evaluated.

4. *Anyone* could attend the meetings, but they didn't ask for _____ advice.

5. *Nobody* cashed the checks, so _____ balance was altered.

Now go back, and circle the words that are simply plural.

EXCEPTION 1: PERSONAL PRONOUNS

12:06 *I, you, he, she, it, we,* and *they* <u>do</u> <u>not</u> follow the rules. They have unique possessive forms. Luckily, most of us are thoroughly familiar with these words.

my house
your house
his house
her house
its house
our house
their house

12:07 Notice that *its*, like *his*, ends with *s* but does not add an apostrophe. *It's* means "it is" or "it has."

English for Professionals

12:08 When the possessive forms of personal pronouns move away from the nouns they modify, most of them end with *s*, but none of them take an apostrophe.

>The house is *mine* (the only one that doesn't end with *s*).
>The house is *yours*.
>The house is *his*.
>The house is *hers*.
>The house is *its*.
>The house is *ours*.
>The house is *theirs*.

12:09 The possessive of *who* is *whose*. (*Who's* means "who is" or "who has" just as *it's* means "it is" or "it has.")

The possessive of *whoever* is *whosever*.

>*Whose* home will win the House Beautiful Contest? *Whosever* home is selected will be awarded $10,000.

PRACTICE 12-D
Fill in the blanks with the possessive forms of the italicized words.
1. I bought *it*, but _____ motor needs extensive repairs.
2. We saw *her* with the books, so we are certain the books are _____.
3. We don't know *who* won the contracts, but we do know _____ bids are in.
4. She asked *him* if she could borrow _____ notes.
5. *They* did, in fact, use visual aids, but these slides are not _____.

Now go back, and circle the words that are simply plural.

12:10 **EXCEPTION 2: WORDS THAT END WITH *S* BUT STILL ADD *'S***
A few words that end with *s* still form the possessive with *'s*. These possessives would sound awkward without the extra syllable that the *'s* adds (the boss's coat, Paris's subways).

12:11 NOTE: In some cases, you might add *'s* where another person would add only an apostrophe, and you would both be correct (Naples' shops or Naples's shops, Mr. Bates' motel or Mr. Bates's motel).

PRACTICE 12-E
Fill in the blanks with the possessive forms of the italicized words.
1. *Mr. Sturgis* has a new car, and _____ new car is electric.
2. The *witness* testified, and the _____ testimony supports our theory.
3. *Los Angeles* has a new mayor, and _____ new mayor is a woman.
4. *Mr. Ross* was in his office, but _____ assistants were not yet there.
5. *Congress* is in session, and _____ critics are having a heyday.

Let your ear be your guide. If your ear calls for an extra syllable, add *'s*. If it doesn't, just add an apostrophe.

12:12 When the possessive of things or animals is awkward, go back to the *of* structure.

>   the house's roof ⟼ the roof of the house
>   Naples's shops or Naples' shops ⟼ the shops of Naples
>   the parenthesis's position or the parenthesis' position ⟼ the position of the parenthesis

EXCEPTION 3: JOINT POSSESSION

12:13 When two or more people or things possess something jointly, only the last person or thing mentioned takes the apostrophe.

>   Earl, Rita, and Julie's new business is going extremely well.
>   Ms. Ore and Mr. Williams' plan has been approved.
>   The suit and tie's designer moved his headquarters to Milan.

12:14 When we replace these people or things with pronouns, we use possessive pronouns for all of them.

>   Barry and Sonia's daughter was born last week.
>   **but**
>   His and her daughter was born last week.

PRACTICE 12-F
Fill in the blanks with the possessive forms of the italicized words.
1. *Steve* and *Carol* bought a new car, but _____ and _____ car isn't ready to be delivered.
2. *Ms. Roy* and *Mr. Hamilton* wrote the ad, and _____ and _____ ad was quite successful.
3. *He* and *she* wrote the ad, and _____ and _____ ad was quite successful.
4. *Sears, IBM,* and *Intel* will work together, and _____, _____, and _____ joint venture should sell quite a few computers.

EXCEPTION 4: PEOPLE'S NAMES THAT END WITH *X* OR *Z*

12:15 When people's names end with *x* or *z*, we often form the possessive by adding only an apostrophe. We treat the *x* or *z* like an *s* (Essex' population, Rafael Hernandez' next vacation).

PRACTICE 12-G
Fill in the blanks with the possessive forms of the italicized words.
1. *Ms. Hamrix* plays a violin that was made in Japan, but _____ bow was made in Germany.
2. Diego *Valázquez* served the Spanish court, and _____ paintings usually depict courtly life.
3. *Dr Stutz* teaches economics, but _____ main interest lies with financial planning.

Let your ear be your guide. If your ear calls for an extra syllable, add *'s*. If it doesn't, just add an apostrophe.

English for Professionals 55

12:16 **EXERCISE 12a**
FORMING POSSESSIVES
Fill in the blanks with the possessive forms of the italicized words.

1. That *girl* has a horse, and the _____ horse is three years old.
2. We tried to fix *it*, but _____ gears are worn out.
3. Our *buses* all have good tires, but the _____ motors need to be serviced.
4. They have a new *couch*, and the _____ arms are hand-carved.
5. *Mr. Rodriguez* is an engineer, and _____ crews build bridges.
6. They have two *dogs*, and the _____ pens are behind those houses.
7. Since *no one* was home, _____ car was damaged when the storms struck.
8. If *you* have a few minutes, we can proofread _____ letters now.
9. A *fox* lives nearby, and we found the _____ den down by those large rocks.
10. The *media* covered the convention, but the _____ reports concentrated on the social events.
11. *Richard* wrote his brother, and within three days, _____ brother was knocking at the door.
12. *Mr. Crow* and *Ms. Lee* have a new store. _____ and _____ new store will open in two weeks.
13. *He* and *she* have a new store. _____ and _____ new store will open in two weeks.
14. The *Smithsons* have a cat, and the _____ cat is named Walter.
15. *We* would probably take better care of the machines if they were _____.
16. We bought a blueberry *bush*, and the _____ canes are already two feet long.
17. *Everyone* had a good time, and _____ dog won at least two ribbons.
18. These *mice* are expensive because the _____ genes carry several rare chromosomes.
19. He didn't say *who* would make the presentations, so we don't know _____ names go in the program.
20. Her *daughter-in-law* was a writer, and her _____ novels were all best-sellers.
21. If *I* can find the deeds, I can prove that the lots are _____.
22. *Whoever* sent the ransom notes remains unknown, but _____ fingerprints are on them will have a few questions to answer.
23. The *Homo sapiens* is a unique creature because the _____ diet is so varied.
24. We tried to help the *men*, but the _____ car just would not start.
25. Those *pens* are of the highest quality, and the _____ manufacturer guarantees them for life.

26. *Someone* left these bags here, and _____ car is parked by the stables.
27. *Ms. Lipschutz* lives in New York, but _____ parents are in Berlin.
28. *Sue* and *Charlie* own a restaurant, and _____ and _____ most famous dish is catfish gumbo.
29. *He* and *she* own a restaurant, and _____ and _____ most famous dish is catfish gumbo.
30. The *cacti* are all healthy, but the _____ blossoms are sparse this year.
31. *Mr. Maddox* was in the US Army, but _____ records have been lost.
32. *Ms. Dobbins* brought a salad, and _____ sons helped her make it.
33. I have read all of her *stories*, and the _____ main characters now seem like old friends.
34. We haven't heard from *anyone*, so we can't say whether _____ computer is on line or not.
35. If *she* likes these colors, we can paint both of _____ houses next week.
36. Both *printers* work well, but the _____ ribbons are worn out.
37. The *oxen* are in the pasture, but the _____ stalls are in that old barn.
38. They know *who* won the race, but they don't know _____ boats came in second and third.
39. Our *school* is new, but our _____ teachers have years of experience.
40. These *films* are expensive, but the _____ vendor will give us a discount.

12:17 **EXERCISE 12b**

APOSTROPHES AND POSSESSIVES

Underline each word that ends with an *s*. Does that word need an apostrophe? If so, does the apostrophe go before or after the *s*? This exercise is difficult because you must be able to tell which words had an *s* before they became possessive and which words did not.

> The novels main character is Huckleberry Finn. Its Huck and Jims ambition to escape civilization and its laws. Its the widows ambition to subject them to society and its rules.
>
> The rivers promise is freedom, so Huck and Jim, civilizations victims, flee on its untamed currents. Each time they go ashore, the runaways are faced with societys ridiculous, cruel, or pathetic behavior, but the runaways refuge is always the savage river. The nations hypocrisy and greed, her citizens inhumanity to man are more terrifying than the cold, blind forces of primeval nature.

Now go back, and circle the words that are simply plural.

13 FREQUENTLY MISUSED WORDS

13:01   Our language is made up of about 340,000 words. Most people understand around 6,000 words but have an active vocabulary of only about 3,000. (Linguists estimate that William Shakespeare had an active vocabulary of about 30,000 words.)

Since we use so few words with any frequency, we inevitably misuse some of them. Review this list of frequently misused words, and study the ones that are difficult for you.

1. *a* and *an*

13:02   Use **an** in front of words that start with a vowel or that sound like they start with a vowel, unless the vowel sound is a long *u* (like the first *u* in *useful* or the *eu* in *euthanasia*). Use *a* in all other situations. (The *o* in words like *one* and *once* sounds like a *w*.)

*A **u**niversity in Ohio bestowed **an** **h**onor on **an** **a**rtist who is **a** **o**ne-time convict and is now in **a** **eu**phoric mood.*

We usually do well with *a* and *an* if we trust our ears, not our eyes.

2. *affect* and *effect*

13:03   *Affect* is a verb (*A* stands for "action"). It means "to change."
Effect is a noun. An *effect* is a thing, like a *sound effect* is a thing.

When you have trouble choosing between *affect* and *effect*, try changing the tense. If different tenses work, it's a verb, and the correct choice is *affect*.

His comments *affected* (*will affect*, *have affected*) bond rates and are certain to have an *effect* (no tense change is possible) on the stock market.

The infinitive (*to affect*) is also a verb.

13:04   CAUTION: *Effect* (*to effect*) is used, rarely, as a verb that means "to bring about."

Will her fresh ideas *effect* (*affected*, *will effect*, *have effected*) a lasting settlement?

3. *amount* and *number*

13:05   *Amount* is preferred for things we measure. *Number* is preferred for things we count.

Increase the *amount* of flour, and decrease the *number* (not *amount*) of eggs.

4. *less* and *fewer*

13:06   *Less* is preferred for things we measure. *Fewer* is preferred for things we count.

Yesterday, we had *less* time and talked to *fewer* (not *less*) people.

5. *anyone*, *any one*, *everyone*, and *every one*

13:07   If the next word is "of," use *any one* or *every one*. If the next word is not "of," use *anyone* or *everyone*. Notice that adding "of" forces us to emphasize the word "one" and write it as a separate word. ("Of" has two letters and forces us to use two words, *any one* or *every one*.)

We could use *any one* (or *every one*) *of* the rooms on this floor if *anyone* (or *everyone*) (no "of") would like to stay here for the discussion.

6. *assure*, *ensure*, and *insure*

13:08   *Assure* means "to make *someone* sure of something." *Ensure* and *insure* mean "to make certain of something." *Assure* is immediately followed by the person or group being assured. *Ensure* isn't. Use *insure* to discuss the insurance industry.

        She called to *assure* us that she is coming.

        She called to *ensure* (or insure) that we *insured* her car against theft.

7. *bad* and *badly*

13:09   Use *bad* to describe people, places, and things (including how you feel). *Badly* describes how something is done. Never *feel badly*, never *feel sadly*, and never *go away madly*. Instead, *feel bad* just as you *feel sad* and *go away mad*. Using *badly* when you should use *bad* is one of the errors of pomposity. (See 18:17.)

        She feels *bad* because she plays golf *badly*.

8. *between* and *among*

13:10   *Between* usually involves two people or things. *Among* usually involves more than two.

        Between you and me, he was *among* the five engineers who botched the project.

9. *each other* and *one another*

13:11   *Each other* usually involves two people or things. *One another* usually involves more than two.

        Sue and Lee kept *each other* informed while the three detectives conferred with *one another* to solve the crime.

10. *can* and *may*

13:12   *Can* refers to the ability to do something. *May* implies permission.

        If you *can* handle a manual shift, you *may* borrow my car.

11. *consensus of opinion*

13:13   *Consensus* means "general opinion." *Consensus of opinion* says it twice. So does *general consensus*.

        The *consensus* of our consultants is that a strike is unnecessary.

12. *different from* and *different than*

13:14   *Different from* is generally preferred over *different than*. One thing might be *bigger than*, *slower than*, or *more suitable than* another, but it's always *different from*. *Than* implies the concept of inferior or superior. *Different from* is simply different.

        Ursula is *different from* her twin brother in that she loves classical music.

13:15   When two people *disagree with* each other, they *differ with* (not *from*) each other.

        They agree with us in matters of politics but *differ with* us in matters of religion.

13. *done* and *already*

Never use *done* when you mean *already*.

I've *already* (not *done*) been there four times today.

Replacing *already* with *done*, like using *ain't*, could mark you as an uneducated person.

14. *every day* and *everyday*

Every day means "each day." Like *each day*, *every day* is two words. *Everyday* means "typical." Like *typical*, *everyday* is one word.

Every day she went to work and enjoyed meeting the *everyday* challenges of business management.

15. *farther* and *further*

Use *farther* for distances. It means more than *far*. Use *further* for intangible things like goals, careers, and purposes. *Further* doesn't refer to distance any more than *fur* does.

The store is *farther* south than the post office.

That stock purchase will *further* his goal of complete ownership.

16. *irregardless*

Irregardless is the property of comics. Use *regardless.*

Regardless (not *Irregardless*) of what he said, we have to be there before noon.

17. *loan* and *lend*

In formal business English, the word *loan* is a noun that refers to borrowed money. *Lend* (*lent, has lent, lending*) is a verb. *Lend* describes the action taken when a lender hands over money to a borrower. *Loan* can be used as a verb, but *lend* is preferred.

He won't *lend* (not *loan*) me the $50 because he already *lent* (not *loaned*) me $100 last week, and I haven't repaid that *loan* yet.

It might help if you remember that people who lend money are called *lenders*, not *loaners*.

18. *majority*

Use *majority* to refer to things with numerous members. *Majority* is plural when it applies to the members in the group. It's singular when it applies to the whole group.

The *majority* of the senators *are* coming, so our party's *majority is* secure.

Do not use *majority* to refer to the larger portion of a single thing.

Most of (not *The majority of*) the meeting was spent working on the budget.

19. *party* and *person*

13:22   *Party* refers to a *person* only in legal contracts and other strictly legal matters. Otherwise, using *party* instead of *person*, *customer*, *individual*, etc is one of the errors of pomposity. (See 18:09.)

> The *person* (or *individual* or *accountant*, not *party*) they hired to audit the accounts interviewed the *party* (or *person* or *employee*) who brought the lawsuit.

20. *people* and *persons*

13:23   The standard plural of *person* is *people*, not *persons*. Using *persons* instead of *people* is one of the errors of pomposity. (See 18:23.)

> The *people* (not *persons*) they hired to audit the accounts interviewed both *parties* (or *people*, not *persons*) involved in the lawsuit.

21. *principal* and *principle*

13:24   *Principal* refers to the main person or thing. *Principles* are rules or guidelines.

> Less than half the payment was applied to the *principal* (main part) of the loan.
> The *principal* (main) reason for this meeting is to elect new officers.
> The *principal* (main teacher) of our school is retiring.
> The *principles* (rules) of free-market economics apply to this case.

22. *real(ly)*, *very*, and *get*

13:25   Because we use these words too often, they are worn out. To use them is to misuse them.

Real(ly) and *very* are words of emphasis, but they have lost their strength.

> "He is *really* a *very* good manager" is less convincing than "He is a good manager."

Dropping *real(ly)* or *very* from a sentence makes the sentence stronger. If you need a word that emphasizes, choose one that is still vigorous.

> "He is an *exceptionally* good manager."

Very with the meaning "exact" is not worn out. (He is the *very* person we met yesterday.)

Get (*got*, *has got*, and *getting*) is the substitute verb. It will stand in for hundreds of verbs.

> "I've *got* to *get* in touch with her before she *gets* to the office" can be improved to read
> "I have to talk with her before she reaches the office."

The *got* in this sentence is unnecessary because *have got* is redundant. (See 18:32.) The two *gets* are less precise than *to talk* or *reaches*. Each time you trade *get* for a more appropriate verb, your choice of words will be more precise.

Occasionally, *get* is unavoidable, as in the expressions "*get* in the car" and "*get* out of bed," but you can easily minimize your use of the word.

23. *sure* and *surely*

Sure means "certain" and *surely* means "certainly."

When you aren't *sure* (certain) whether you should use *sure* or *surely*, try substituting *certain* or *certainly*, and you will *surely* (certainly) make the correct choice.

24. *that* and *which*

Many, but not all, good writers differentiate between *that* and *which*. If you follow these rules, you will not overuse either word. (Use *who* and *whom*, not *that* and *which*, to refer to people.)

That is used to start most dependent clauses. We sometimes drop *that* from sentences.

The truck *that* I drove ran well. (The truck I drove ran well.)

The house *that* won the award is on Third Street. (*That* can't be dropped.)

Which is used only when the dependent clause is an interrupter (comma Rule Four). We never drop *which*.

Wright's Kaufmann House, *which* he designed in 1936, is one of his best.

Her new Ford truck, *which* came in today, runs beautifully.

The occasional misuse of *which* is hardly worth noticing. The habitual misuse of *which* is one of the *errors of pomposity*. (See 18:11.)

25. *lay*, *lie*, *set*, and *sit*

Many people think these words are impossible to use correctly. Without doubt, they are our most frequently misused words.

To avoid confusion, learn that *lay* and *set* mean "to put" (or "put in place"). *Lie* and *sit* don't mean "to put" (or "put in place"). Their tenses work this way:

PUT

PRESENT	Please *lay* or *set* (put) the books on the table.
SIMPLE PAST	Yesterday he *laid* or *set* (put) the books on the table.
PAST BUILT WITH *HAVE*	He *has laid* or we *have set* (put) them there for days.
THE *-ING* FORM	He is *laying* or *setting* (putting) them on the table.

NOT PUT

PRESENT	Please *lie* or *sit* (not put) there until you feel better.
SIMPLE PAST	He *lay* or *sat* (not put) there until he felt better.
PAST BUILT WITH *HAVE*	He *has lain* or we *have sat* (not put) there for days.
THE *-ING* FORM	His hat is *lying* or *sitting* (not putting) over there.

Lay and *set* (like *put*) involve one thing doing something to another. *Lie* and *sit* are what something does all by itself.

You will choose the correct words if you follow these two steps:

13:29 **STEP 1**
Memorize this chart by writing it again and again (without the headings PRESENT, SIMPLE PAST, etc). Keep a copy of it handy until you know it by heart.

	PUT (or *put in place*)	*NOT PUT*
PRESENT	lay • set	lie • sit
SIMPLE PAST	laid • set	lay • sat
PAST BUILT WITH *HAVE*	(have) laid • (have) set	(have) lain • (have) sat
THE *-ING* FORM	laying • setting	lying • sitting

13:30 **STEP 2**
Read the sentence in question. Ask yourself, "Does the word *put* (or *put in place*) work here?"

If the answer is *YES*, go to the *PUT* list.

If the answer is *NO*, go to the *NOT PUT* list.

13:31 Can you choose the correct word in the following sentences?

1. She has **(laid, lain)** out in the sun all afternoon.

   Does this sentence involve the person *putting* something? *NO*. Go to the *NOT PUT* list. The correct choice is *lain*.

2. During recess, the child **(sets, sits)** her books under the desk.

   Is the child *putting* something? *YES*. Go to the *PUT* list. The correct choice is *sets*.

3. The computer is **(setting, sitting)** on the table.

   Is the computer *putting* something? *NO*. Go to the *NOT PUT* list. The correct choice is *sitting*.

4. Have they **(laid, lain)** the bricks yet?

   Does the word *put* work here? No, **but put in place** does. Go to the *PUT* list. The correct choice is *laid*.

   PRACTICE 13-A
   Circle the correct word.

   1. He was so weak that he **(laid, lay)** down on the ground.

   2. Please **(set, sit)** these letters on the hall table.

   3. Are those notes, the ones **(laying, lying)** on the shelf, hers?

   4. Yesterday, he **(sat, set)** the report on my desk.

   5. You should **(lay, lie)** down until your head clears.

English for Professionals

6. Last week, he **(laid, lay)** his coat on that table.

7. The paper has been **(laying, lying)** there all day.

8. He wants to **(lay, lie)** out by the pool tomorrow.

9. That lamp has **(sat, set)** there for three weeks.

10. She has **(laid, lain)** all the tiles around the bathtub.

11. Monday, he **(sat, set)** by the window and read.

12. She was **(laying, lying)** her scarf on the bench.

13. He has **(sat, set)** up a schedule that suits all of us.

14. Don't **(lay, lie)** the blanket on the bed.

15. Sue is **(setting, sitting)** the bowl by the window.

13:32 **EXERCISE 13**
FREQUENTLY MISUSED WORDS
Circle the preferred word or phrase.

1. **(Most, The majority)** of the water is stored in the holding ponds.

2. The **(consensus, consensus of opinion, general consensus)** is that we will win.

3. Sundays, he always **(lays, lies)** on the sofa and reads the paper.

4. They **(assured, ensured, insured)** us that we have their support.

5. **(Can, May)** we see him now or has he **(already, done)** left?

6. A **(real, really, very)** large percentage of the **(people, persons)** in our class did well.

7. He has **(sat, set)** a limit on our expenditures.

8. The car we **(lent, loaned)** him **(averages, gets)** 30 miles per gallon.

9. Did **(any one, anyone)** check the mail **(every day, everyday)**?

10. Did **(any one, anyone)** of you think of the **(every day, everyday)** customer's needs?

11. Go about one mile **(farther, further)**, and turn right.

12. The report has **(laid, lain)** on his desk for three days.

13. If we had **(fewer, less)** options, the decision would be easier.

14. George and Juanita differed **(from, with)** each other because his approach to economics is different **(from, than)** hers.

15. **(Irregardless, Regardless)** of how we feel, we must go to the meeting.

16. Every cigar he lights **(sets, sits)** in the ashtray and burns down to a stub.

17. He will **(sure, surely)** be pleased when he hears the news.

18. I want to encourage more cooperation **(among, between)** the two of us.

19. The **(principal, principle)** of the loan is $20,000.

20. She was **(setting, sitting)** at a bus stop with a magazine in her hand.

21. We need to increase the **(amount, number)** of training sessions.

22. We need to increase the **(amount, number)** of training our employees receive.

23. He found **(a, an)** unique solution to the problem **(that, which)** has plagued us for years.

24. They understand the **(principals, principles)** of management.

25. Every Sunday afternoon, he **(lays, lies)** out by the pool.

26. We want to **(assure, ensure, insure)** that he will have a chance to see her.

27. He has met the **(party, person)** who bought the new mowers.

28. She was the **(principal, principle)** force behind the merger.

29. They **(sat, set)** the quitclaim on her desk.

30. His philosophy had a major **(affect, effect)** on our work.

31. **(Every one, Everyone)** of you would have drawn the same conclusion.

32. **(Every one, Everyone)** here would have drawn the same conclusion.

33. He is **(laying, lying)** around the house instead of looking for a job.

34. Would **(lending, loaning)** the Senator that much money be unethical?

35. The money was divided equally **(among, between)** the three boys.

36. He is attending night school to **(farther, further)** his chances for advancement.

37. The change in the prime rate **(affected, effected)** the market.

38. After he spoke for **(a, an)** half **(a, an)** hour, **(a, an)** one-man band started to play.

39. The software he **(bought, got)** in New York is **(real, really, very)** effective.

40. Mrs. Robinson was the **(principal, principle)** of our school.

41. My parents gave **(each other, one another)** a new stereo for Christmas.

42. Please remind him to **(ensure, insure)** the new company car.

43. In the field, our technicians and engineers work closely with **(each other, one another)**.

44. We hope your advice will have an **(affect, effect)** on his attitude.

45. We hope your advice will **(affect, effect)** a change in his attitude.

46. He is well educated, but he is **(unprincipaled, unprincipled)**.

47. His proposal, **(that, which)** I delivered this morning, **(sure, surely)** was well written.

48. They have **(done, already)** mailed the report.

49. Please **(lie, lay)** this memorandum on her desk.

50. If he feels **(bad, badly)** about what he said, he should apologize.

14 SPELLING

14:01 The English language is easy to speak, but its words are often difficult to spell. In many other languages, German and Spanish for example, almost all words are easy to spell because they are written exactly as they are pronounced.

In English, spelling and pronunciation are often mismatched (consider ***tough***, ***bough***, and ***through***). As a result, we find ourselves memorizing difficult spellings or trying to picture words in the absence of sound. Americans who can confidently spell any word they have ever seen, Mark Twain for example, often become folk heroes. In Germany or in Spain, the average citizen could do as well.

English is difficult to spell because it's a stew consisting of one part French, one part Anglo-Saxon, and dashes of other languages thrown in for flavor. To make matters worse, the spelling of most words became standardized four or five hundred years ago when printing presses were introduced. Since then, pronunciation has changed considerably.

Unfortunately, we are stuck with a language that is hard to spell. Never apologize for being a weak speller. The problem is with our language, not with your brain.

A few good spellers take pleasure in belittling poor spellers. When you meet one of these bores, relax, lean back, and throw out a few of the common words almost no one can spell (try ***curriculum***, ***hors d'oeuvre***, ***hemorrhoid***, ***bureaucracy***, or ***prerogative***). Don't pretend. Be prepared to spell any word you mention. Unless you've stumbled upon a true folk hero, your critic will hurry to change the subject.

Linguists know that poor spelling is no proof of weak intelligence, but poor spelling can be one sign of a sloppy intellect. Our language is difficult to spell, but we are blessed with the dictionary. Use it. When in doubt, look up the word. If you are not a proficient speller, you can at least be a conscientious proofreader.

THE TEN MOST FREQUENTLY MISSPELLED WORDS

14:02 Like using ***ain't***, misspelling these words suggests to others that you are poorly educated. Study them carefully and ***never*** misspell them again.

14:03 1. ***a lot***
These two words are ***NEVER*** written as one word. If they were, we couldn't use the phrase "a whole lot."

14:04 2. ***all right***
These two words are ***NEVER*** written as one word. The word ***alright*** does not exist in standard English.

14:05 3. ***calendar***
The last two letters are ***ar***, not ***er***.

14:06 4. ***cannot***
When can and not are combined, they are ***ALWAYS*** written as one word.

14:07 5. *February*

If you pronounce it correctly, you won't misspell it.

14:08 6. *you're* and *your*

You're is a contraction of *you are*. *Your* is the possessive form of *you*.

14:09 7. *it's* and *its*

These words are often misspelled because people confuse their meanings.

It's is a contraction of the words *it is* or *it has*, just as *isn't* is a contraction of *is not*.

Its is the possessive form of *it*. Remember that none of the possessive personal pronouns (neither *hers, his, ours, theirs, yours,* nor *its*) use apostrophes. (See 12:06-07.)

14:10 8. *separate*

Some people say this word is misspelled more often than any other in our language. It's never spelled *sep*e*rate*. It's always spelled *sep*a*rate*. (There's *a rat* in it.)

14:11 9. *their*, *there*, and *they're*

Many people confuse these three words.

Their is the possessive form of *they*.

Their mutt bit me on the leg.

There is a pointing word.

He is over *there*.

Sometimes, *there* seems to point off into the air.

There are two reasons I called.

They're is a contraction of the words *they are*.

They're (They are) willing to meet us half way.

14:12 10. *to* and *too*

These words have different meanings. Unless *to* is tied to a verb ("*To err* is human, *to forgive* divine"), it usually means "toward." *Too* has two meanings, "also" and "excessively."

To and *too* are also pronounced differently when they are used in sentences. *Too* rhymes with *blue*. *To* usually rhymes with uh. The only time *to* rhymes with *blue* is when it falls at the end of a sentence.

Too Tall Jones wants *to* go *to* the movies *too*.
(blue)   (uh) (uh)   (blue)

English for Professionals

GUIDELINES FOR AVOIDING OTHER COMMON MISSPELLINGS

Experts have come up with countless rules to help us spell English words correctly. The following three rules are, perhaps, the only ones that are reasonably reliable.

14:13   A. Use *i* before *e*, except after *c* and in words that sound like **neighbor** or **weigh**.

(Use *i* before *e*) believe, grieve, die, field, pierce, sieve, tie

(except after *c*) perceive, deceit, receive

(and in words that sound like **neighbor** and **weigh**.) heinous, vein

14:14   B. When a word ends with *e* and we add a suffix to it, we drop the *e* if the suffix starts with a vowel. We keep the *e* if the suffix starts with a consonant.

biodegrade + able = biodegradable

come + ing = coming

engage + ment = engagement

tire + less = tireless

14:15   C. When a one-syllable word ends with a **consonant-vowel-consonant** pattern and we add a suffix that starts with a vowel, we double the final letter.

sip + ed = sipped

stop + er = stopper

14:16   This guideline applies to words with more than one syllable *if* we stress the last syllable.

propel + er = propeller

confer + ing = conferring

EXERCISE 14
SPELLING

I. Ask a friend to read the following nonsensical paragraph to you, and write it down as if you were taking dictation. Your reader may repeat the sentences as often as necessary.

> Even though the *calendar* month of *February* is coming and *there* are *a lot* of *separate* benefits, we *cannot* predict *its* weather. Next Wednesday, *you're* going *to their* house *too*, and I'm certain that *they're all right* if *it's your* idea.

When you finish, check your spelling. If you misspelled any of the italicized words, study them carefully until you are confident that you will never misspell them again.

Remember, misspelling one of these words, like using *ain't*, could mark you as an uneducated person.

II. In the blank by each example, give the letter of the guideline that determines the spelling or the shift in spelling. If the word is an exception to the rule, write *EX* in the blank along with the letter of the rule it disobeys.

1. _____ freight
2. _____ occur ⟼ occurring
3. _____ receipt
4. _____ cure ⟼ curable
5. _____ confer ⟼ conferring
6. _____ rid ⟼ ridding
7. _____ flame ⟼ flameproof
8. _____ submit ⟼ submitting
9. _____ move ⟼ movable
10. _____ protein
11. _____ chief
12. _____ forbid ⟼ forbidden
13. _____ sleigh
14. _____ prefer ⟼ preferred
15. _____ conceit
16. _____ trouble ⟼ troublesome
17. _____ their
18. _____ care ⟼ careful
19. _____ brief
20. _____ begin ⟼ beginning
21. _____ piece
22. _____ hop ⟼ hopping
23. _____ pipe ⟼ pipeline
24. _____ cut ⟼ cutting
25. _____ mile ⟼ mileage

15 HYPHENATING COMPOUND ADJECTIVES

15:01　Sometimes, hyphens join words even when dictionaries don't list the words as hyphenated. In most cases, such hyphenated words are *compound adjectives*.

When two or more words function as a single adjective, they are called *compound adjectives*, and they are usually, but not always, hyphenated. Hyphenating compound adjectives can be tricky. Don't leave this chapter without reading the "Words of Caution" (15:21-24).

Before we discuss compound adjectives, we need to define two terms, *adjective* and *complement adjective*.

WHAT IS AN ADJECTIVE?

15:02　An *adjective* is a word that modifies a noun (a person, place, or thing). An adjective describes something or someone and answers the question *what kind of* or *which one*. Most adjectives stand in front of the nouns they modify.

> The *young* man drove a *broken-down* car.

Which man? The *young* one. What kind of car? A *broken-down* car.

In this example, *young* and *broken-down* are adjectives. They describe *man* and *car*.

NOTE: *Young*, like most adjectives, is a single word. However, *broken-down* is a single adjective made by combining two words. It's not a *broken* car, and it's not a *down* car. It's a *broken-down* car. *Broken-down* is a *compound adjective*.

PRACTICE 15-A

Circle the adjectives.
1. Their mean dog bit the new mailman.
2. A part-time employee works in the other office.
3. A well-dressed woman stood at the iron gate.
4. The lucky man won a 50-foot yacht.

WHAT IS A COMPLEMENT ADJECTIVE?

15:03　A *complement adjective* describes or modifies the subject of a sentence but is placed after the verb. (Another name for a *complement adjective* is *predicate adjective*.)

> The man　is　young.
> SUBJ　VERB　C ADJ

> The car　is　broken-down.
> SUBJ　VERB　C ADJ

> William Cobb　was　healthy.
> SUBJ　　　　VERB　C ADJ

> She　was　even-tempered.
> SUBJ　VERB　　C ADJ

Young describes *the man*, *broken-down* describes *the car*, *healthy* describes William Cobb, and *even-tempered* describes whoever *she* is. Because these words describe (modify) nouns, they are adjectives. They answer the questions *what kind of* or *which one*.

Why are they called *complement adjectives*? If we drop the adjectives from these sentences, the sentences lose their meaning. Writing "The man is" makes no sense. The word *complement* means "to complete." Because such adjectives come after the verbs and complete the sentences, they are most frequently called *complement adjectives*.

(Some people call complement adjectives *predicate adjectives* because these adjectives come after the verb, and *predicate* is another name for *verb*.)

15:04 Usually, the verb that separates the noun from its complement adjective will be some form of the verb *to be* (*am, are, is, was, were, have been, will be,* etc). If the verb is not a form of *to be*, it will be a verb like *seem, appear, look,* or *act*.

```
The man    seems    young.
 SUBJ      VERB     C ADJ

The car    appears   broken-down.
 SUBJ       VERB       C ADJ

William Cobb   looked   healthy.
   SUBJ         VERB    C ADJ

She   acted   even-tempered.
SUBJ  VERB       C ADJ
```

Notice that writing "The man seems" makes no sense. That sentence needs a complement adjective like *young* to complete it and give it meaning. Notice also that *seem, appear, look,* and *act* incorporate the meaning of *to be*. We could have written "seems *to be*," "appears *to be*," "looked as if he *was*," and "acted as if she *was*."

TESTING FOR COMPLEMENT ADJECTIVES

15:05 To test for a complement adjective, take the suspected complement adjective, and place it in front of the subject.

The *young* man is (seems) *young*.
The *broken-down* car is (appears) *broken-down*.

These sentences might be ridiculous, but they demonstrate that *young* and *broken-down* make sense in either position. Since *young* and *broken-down* make sense in front of the noun and after the verb, you know that they serve as complement adjectives when they follow the verb.

Try the same test on "The captain is *our sponsor*."

The *our sponsor* captain is *our sponsor*.

Using *our sponsor* in front of *captain* doesn't work, so *our sponsor* is not a complement adjective.

This test does not work well with people's names or with pronouns.

Healthy William Cobb was *healthy*.
Even-tempered she was *even-tempered*.

We don't ordinarily put adjectives in front of names and pronouns. The test does work if we replace *William Cobb* and *she* with common nouns like *the man* and *the woman*.

> The *healthy* man was *healthy*.
> The *even-tempered* woman was *even-tempered*.

Healthy and *even-tempered*, like young and *broken-down*, are adjectives. They describe *William Cobb* and *she*. The only difference between complement adjectives and other adjectives is that complement adjectives are placed after the verb.

NOTE: *Young* and *healthy*, like most adjectives, are single words. *Broken-down* and *even-tempered* are *compound adjectives* made by combining two words.

PRACTICE 15-B
Circle the complement adjectives.
1. Their dog is mean.
2. One of their employees was part-time.
3. She always acts high-strung.
4. Carlos Gomez felt lucky.
5. Their house is a mansion.

COMPOUND ADJECTIVES

15:06   Now that you understand the terms *adjective* and *complement adjective*, we will concentrate on <u>*compound adjectives*</u> and <u>*compound* complement adjectives</u>.

When two or more words function as a single adjective, that single adjective is called a *compound adjective*.

Compound adjectives, like single-word adjectives, are used two ways. They serve as normal adjectives when they appear in front of nouns, and they serve as complement adjectives when they follow the verb. Either way, *compound adjectives* are usually, but not always, hyphenated.

We will look at these two types of *compound adjectives*. In addition, we will mention *compound adjectives* formed with *numbers*, with *well* and *ill*, and with *self* and *ex*.

1. COMPOUND ADJECTIVES THAT PRECEDE NOUNS

15:07   When two or more words precede a noun and function as a single adjective, hyphenate them. Certain exceptions to this rule will be discussed under EXCEPTIONS (15:13-19).

> She prepared the *end-of-the-month* report and then attended an *all-day* seminar.

When *end-of-the-month* precedes the noun *report*, it tells us "which report." When *all-day* precedes the noun *seminar*, it tells us "what kind of seminar." They are *compound adjectives* and they are **hyphenated**.

15:08   Sometimes, compound adjectives are broken apart to avoid repetition.

> Our *long-* and *short-term* investments are doing well.

2. COMPOUNDS WITH NUMBERS

15:09   Compounds with numbers are hyphenated when they precede nouns. (See *Exception 5* [15:17].)

The *50-year-old* man took a *two-week* vacation to prepare for the *100-meter* dash.

NOTE: Words like *year*, *week*, and *meter* remain singular in compound adjectives. Elsewhere, they would be plural.

The man is *50 years* old, and he spent *two weeks* preparing for a race of *100 meters*.

3. COMPOUNDS WITH *WELL* AND *ILL*

15:10   Compounds built with *well* and *ill* are always hyphenated when they precede nouns. (They are sometimes hyphenated when they serve as complement adjectives. See *Exception 7* [15:19].)

A *well-known* consultant reorganized their *ill-conceived* project.

4. COMPOUND ADJECTIVES FORMED WITH THE PREFIXES *SELF* AND *EX*

15:11   When you build compounds with the prefixes *self* and *ex*, hyphenate them no matter where they stand.

self-assured, self-made, self-taught, ex-president, ex-wife, ex-husband

In fact, all words that use *self* as a prefix are hyphenated (*self-esteem, self-confidence, self-portrait,* but not *selfish* and not *selfless*).

PRACTICE 15-C
Add the hyphens.

1. Her blue green eyes were hiding behind sunglasses.
2. A three to five day seminar could easily cover the topic.
3. Her all female team won the tournament.
4. A well dressed, self confident sales representative entered the room.

5. COMPOUND COMPLEMENT ADJECTIVES

15:12   When two words function as a single complement adjective, hyphenate them. Certain exceptions to this rule will be discussed under EXCEPTIONS (15:13-19).

Howard is *long-legged*.
(The *long-legged* man is *long-legged*.)

They seemed *close-knit*.
(The *close-knit* family(?) seemed *close-knit*.)

Any house in that neighborhood will be *high-priced*.
(Any *high-priced* house will be *high-priced*.)

Long-legged describes *Howard*, *close-knit* describes whoever *they* are, and *high-priced* tells us what kind of *house*. They are compound adjectives and they are hyphenated.

PRACTICE 15-D
Add the hyphens.

1. Her eyes looked blue green.
2. The seminar will be first rate.
3. The team that won was all female.
4. He is even tempered.

English for Professionals

SEVEN EXCEPTIONS
In seven cases, words that appear to be compound adjectives are not hyphenated.

15:13   *Exception 1*: Do not hyphenate two words if the first one ends with *ly*.

>   The *carefully planned* meeting went well.
>   The woman was *beautifully dressed*.
>
>   *Carefully planned* and *beautifully dressed* seem to pass our test for compound adjectives. (The *carefully planned* meeting was *carefully planned*.) Still, the *ly* ending kills the hyphen.

15:14   *Exception 2*: Don't hyphenate two words if the first or the second word is possessive.

>   Every month, he saved *two weeks'* wages.
>   That report is the *state auditor's*. (The state auditor wrote it.)
>   The *boys' team* roster is on the bulletin board.
>
>   *Two weeks'* tells us what kind of *wages*, *state auditor's* tells us which *report*, and *boy's team* modifies *roster*. These words act like compound adjectives but are not hyphenated.

15:15   *Exception 3*: Do not hyphenate two or more words commonly used to name a single thing.

>   After earning her *high school* diploma, she worked as our *Human Resources* director and later became an *Academy Award* winner.
>
>   *High school* and *Academy Award* are single things. *Human Resources* is a single department. When such words are used as adjectives, they are not hyphenated.

15:16   *Exception 4*: Compound adjectives with three or more words are hyphenated *only* when they fall in front of the words they modify. Do not hyphenate complement adjectives with three or more words.

>   Her *off-the-record* comments were interesting.
>   **but**
>   Her comments were *off the record*.

15:17   *Exception 5*: Do not hyphenate compounds with the word *percent*.

>   Their broker projected a *10 percent* return on the investment.

15:18   *Exception 6*: Do not hyphenate compounds with numbers unless they precede the words they modify. (See 15:09.)

>   That little girl caught a *three-pound* catfish.
>   **but**
>   The catfish weighed *three pounds*.

73

15:19 *Exception 7*: Do not hyphenate compound *complement* adjectives built with *well* and *ill* unless that hyphenated compound is listed in your dictionary (*Merriam-Webster* is the best place to look).

> A *well-trained* soldier lead the *ill-fated* expedition.
> **but**
> Their leader was *well trained*, but the expedition was *ill-fated*.

Ill-fated is in *Merriam-Webster*, but *well-trained* is not.

15:20 NOTE: Actually, this exception applies to any two-word complement adjective if the first of the two words could be an adverb. If you are curious and if you understand traditional grammar, you can go to *Gregg* for a thorough explanation. Meanwhile, *Exception 7* will prevent you from making the most common errors.

PRACTICE 15-E
Add the hyphens.
1. Our five year contract gives us a 4 percent raise.
2. Our income producing investments are listed on those income tax forms.
3. Their well designed headquarters building is also well built.
4. Her day to day summaries are made to order.
5. His old world charm was responsible for his new book's success.
6. Those tax exempt bonds gave us some desperately needed security.
7. Their 6 foot long rope should have been 12 feet long.
8. For a self made millionaire, he certainly is self conscious.
9. Our hard won victory will soon be well known.

WORDS OF CAUTION
Four pitfalls await writers who are learning to hyphenate compound adjectives.

15:21 1. Be careful not to hyphenate single-word adjectives that precede two-word nouns.

> An *antique-duck* decoy (incorrect, no hyphen)
> A *slow-moving* van (incorrect? no hyphen?)

In the first example, we have a *duck decoy* that is an *antique* (an antique-duck decoy would attract only antique ducks). In the second example, the hyphen is correct if we have a *van* that is *moving slowly*. It's incorrect if we have a *moving van* that is *slow*.

15:22 2. Be on the lookout for compound adjectives that have evolved into single words.

> He feels *light-headed*, but he is *lighthearted*.

We might expect *lighthearted*, like *light-headed*, to be hyphenated, but *lighthearted* has evolved into a single word. Similarly, *upper-case* letters are now *uppercase* letters, and your *long-time* friends have become *longtime* friends.

You are fairly safe when you hyphenate compound adjectives made up of randomly selected words (*helium-filled* balloon, *four-year-old* child), but when your compound adjective sounds like a standard expression, check your dictionary. (*Merriam-Webster* is the best place to look.)

English for Professionals

15:23   3. Do not place a hyphen between the adjective and the noun it modifies.

She signed a *two-year* contract (not a *two-year-contract*).

15:24   4. Do not hyphenate prefixes like *pre*, *non*, and *over* unless *Merriam-Webster* clearly indicates that they should be hyphenated. The only prefixes commonly hyphenated are *ex* and *self*. (See 15:11.) Prefixes used with numbers are also hyphenated, as are prefixes attached to capitalized words and prefixes that could cause a word to be misread.

He is a *nonsmoker* in his *mid-thirties*, but he *overcooked* the beans that our *un-American ex-president* bought for the *re-creation* of a colonial meal.

CAUTION: Most computer spelling checkers recognize common words that start with prefixes (like *nonsmoker*), but they don't recognize uncommon words that start with prefixes (like *nonterminal*) and flag them as "misspelled." If the user adds a hyphen, the computer then accepts the word, creating the false impression that the hyphen represents proper usage. *Do not trust your spelling checker when you are dealing with prefixes.*

15:25   **EXERCISE 15**
HYPHENATING COMPOUND ADJECTIVES

Add the hyphens. If you would have to check *Merriam-Webster* before adding a hyphen, place a question mark (?) where the hyphen might go. In the first ten sentences, the critical parts of the sentences have been underlined for you.

1. We applied for a two year extension on our 4 percent loan.
2. The hand made chess set came from a South American country.
3. Three well known physicians have already seen her.
4. Being self conscious, George felt light headed.
5. Her up to date information was, in fact, up to date.
6. He is a non smoker so his bride didn't ask for a pre nuptial agreement.
7. They make reservations on a first come, first served basis.
8. The maintenance workers' responsibilities are well understood.
9. According to our corporate financial advisor, all gifts to Tom's home are tax deductible.
10. The 50, 75, and 100 foot hoses are guaranteed for five years.
11. To buy a worn out farm, they applied for a 20 or 25 year loan and are hoping for a 12 percent interest rate.
12. She brought a three layered cake to the New Year's Eve party.
13. In spite of their ill advised personnel policies, their employees were well balanced and had high self esteem.
14. His comments will have no effect on self respecting employees who are high spirited.
15. Her plans are well designed, and a highly qualified engineer has approved them.
16. We found a carefully written note on the new employee's desk.
17. Her well known exmother-in-law is self employed and owns an interior decorating firm.
18. Their foreign born president took power at the end of the month.

19. They concluded that our 8 percent markup is cost effective.
20. Major Anderson ordered a seven day a week, around the clock watch over the fort for three months.
21. She might be ill tempered, but she is still a highly respected professional.
22. As far as her informal support group was concerned, her suggestions were ill advised.
23. Our make shift radio can't pick up the high and low range frequencies.
24. When she found her long lost son, he was working with a Nobel Prize winning physicist.
25. That brightly painted car is a customized hot rod.
26. Joe passed the civil service exam and will work in the word processing department.
27. Did the young well digger order his favorite side dish?
28. The community based project lead to a new found sense of security.
29. The five and six year olds were ill prepared to deal with the crisis.
30. Their well planned attack lasted only six hours.
31. A self educated surveyor laid out the plot, but he made a 0.8 percent error when he calculated the acreage.
32. The cautiously constructed constitution required that all presidents be native born.
33. The old car's engine was out of commission.
34. Her common sense approach seemed to be ready made to solve our problem.
35. When the out of control crowd surged forward, the soldiers went out of control too.
36. Our conference lasted three days, and we studied both high and low tech approaches to personnel management.
37. The Norwegian anti defamation league met in mid winter.
38. His ill gotten gains are ill deserved.
39. That so called ten year project was completed in eight years.
40. That elegantly dressed woman is a Georgia Tech professor.
41. A well nourished dog was eating the young man's lunch.
42. A plotter that is computer driven designed the self addressed envelope.
43. Our easy going coach wears a sweat stained uniform.
44. The propane and diesel filled containers must be moved to the new storage facility.
45. Her high school principal attended a three hour long presentation on math anxiety.
46. Our exdirector was well equipped and self assured.
47. The heavily wooded hillside hid an ill constructed barn.
48. This wall is steel reinforced and gives us a 70 percent increase in blast control.
49. Last year's report was 40 pages long.
50. A twenty year old woman asked a well heeled real estate agent about his second and third floor apartments and the self igniting ovens that the cost of living patrol recommends so highly.

16 THE SUBJUNCTIVE

16:01 Have you ever said, "If I *were* a millionaire, I *would* do things my way," "*May* he *rest* in peace," or "They *insist* that we *be* on time"? If so, you have used the **subjunctive mood**. The **subjunctive** is a form of expression few people understand, yet we use it correctly almost all the time.

Our mistakes occur when we use the subjunctive to discuss things *contrary to fact* (when we express our dreams or speculate about what might be or what might have been).

UNDERSTANDING THE SUBJUNCTIVE
We use the subjunctive to discuss things *contrary to fact* in two distinct cases, in *wishes* and in *if-would* sentences.

WISHES
16:02 One simple use of the subjunctive occurs when we make wishes.

> I wish I *were* rich so I *could* sail across the ocean (but I am not rich, and I cannot sail across the ocean).

> We wish we *had* a reliable car so we *could* drive to Quebec (but we don't have a reliable car, and we cannot drive to Quebec).

> He wishes he *worked* here so he *could* move up faster (but he doesn't work here, and he can't move up faster).

16:03 Frequently, we express our wishes without adding the *so* clauses.

> I wish I *were* rich (but I'm not).

> We wish we *had* a reliable car (but we don't).

> He wishes he *worked* here (but he doesn't).

These examples are in the present tense. We also can wish in the future tense (I wish we *would* buy a new car) and in the past tense (she wishes she *had taken* that job).

IF-WOULD SENTENCES
16:04 We also use the subjunctive to discuss things we *would* do under certain conditions.

> *If* I *were* rich, I *would* (or *could* or *might*) sail across the ocean (but I am not rich, and I will not [cannot, may not] sail across the ocean).

> We *would* (or *could* or *might*) drive to Quebec *if* we *had* a reliable car (but we will not [cannot, may not] drive to Quebec because we don't have a reliable car).

> *If* he *worked* here, he *would* (or *could* or *might*) move up faster (but he doesn't work here, so he will not [cannot, may not] move up faster).

Unless you are a serious students of grammar, skip 16:05 and 16:06, and go on to 16:07.

To build the subjunctive, follow these steps.

16:05 **PRESENT TENSE**
STEP 1: Select the present tense of the verb that goes with the pronoun *we*. Then move back one step in time.

    we are ⟼ we *were*   we have ⟼ we *had*

    we live ⟼ we *lived*   we swim ⟼ we *swam*

STEP 2: Apply this verb form to all present-tense situations.

if I *were*	if I *had*	if I *lived*	if I *swam*
if you *were*	if you *had*	if you *lived*	if you *swam*
if he *were*	if he *had*	if he *lived*	if he *swam*
if we *were*	if we *had*	if we *lived*	if we *swam*
if they *were*	if they *had*	if they *lived*	if they *swam*

STEP 3: Use these verb forms to make wishes and to build present-tense *if-would* sentences with *would*, *could*, or *might*.

    I wish I *were* his father.
    If he *had* his notes, he *could* give you all the details.
    We *would* eat cheese every day *if* we *lived* in France.
    If they *swam* more often, they *might* be in better shape.

Remember, the key to selecting the correct subjunctive verb is to use the verb that goes with the pronoun *we*.

16:06 **PAST TENSE**
STEP 1: Start with the past tense of the verb that uses *have*, and change the *have* to its subjunctive form, *had*.

    we have been ⟼ we *had been*   we have had ⟼ we *had had*

    we have lived ⟼ we *had lived*   we have swum ⟼ we *had swum*

STEP 2: Apply this verb form to all past-tense situations.

if I *had been*	if I *had had*	if I *had lived*	if I *had swum*
if you *had been*	if you *had had*	if you *had lived*	if you *had swum*
if he *had been*	if he *had had*	if he *had lived*	if he *had swum*
if we *had been*	if we *had had*	if we *had lived*	if we *had swum*
if they *had been*	if they *had had*	if they *had lived*	if they *had swum*

STEP 3: Use these verb forms to make wishes in the past tense or to build past-tense *if-would* sentences with *would*, *could* or *might*.

    I wish I *had been* his father.
    If he *had had* his notes, he *could have* given you all the details.
    We *would have* eaten cheese every day *if* we *had lived* in France.
    If they *had swum* more often, they *might have* been in better shape.

English for Professionals

ERRORS INVOLVING THE SUBJUNCTIVE

Using the subjunctive is simple, but many writers make three serious errors with it. We will discuss these three errors, and we will mention the awkward repetition of *had*.

ERROR ONE: USING *WAS* INSTEAD OF *WERE*

16:07 Many people write sentences like these examples:

If I *was* rich (incorrect, use *were*), I would sail across the ocean.

She wishes she *was* able to help you (incorrect, use *were*).

I would tell her a thing or two if I *was* you (incorrect, use *were*).

This error is so common that some experts now consider it acceptable, but most good writers still use *were*.

All subjunctive verbs behave as if the subject were *we*. (See 16:05.) People who understand that subjunctive verb forms are tied to the pronoun *we*, find "I wish I was rich" as inappropriate as "We was rich."

PRACTICE 16-A
Correct the following sentences.
1. What would Maria do if her car (think *we*) was not running well?
2. If he (think *we*) was here, he could fix it.
3. I wish you (think *we*) was my supervisor.
4. If the wind was stronger, we would fly the kite.
5. She could have the position if she was trained in surveying.
6. "I wish I was a teddy bear."

ERROR TWO: USING *OF* INSTEAD OF *HAVE*

16:08 In casual conversations, we often drop the *h* from *have* and say *'ave*, which sounds like *of*. We then take our careless pronunciation to the written word and write sentences like the following examples:

If I had been rich, I would *of* sailed across the ocean (incorrect, use *have*).

We could *of* driven to Quebec (incorrect, use *have*) if we had had a reliable car.

If she had worked here, she might *of* moved up faster (incorrect, use *have*).

PRACTICE 16-B
Correct the following sentences.
1. If I had been there, I might of been of assistance.
2. She could of stayed longer if she had accumulated more vacation days.
3. If they had been earlier, they would of had plenty to eat.

ERROR THREE: USING *MIGHT COULD*

16:09   In *if-would* sentences, use *would*, *could*, or *might*, but do not combine *might* and *could*.

INCORRECT: If she worked here, she *might could* move up faster.

CORRECT: If she worked here, she *could* (or *would* or *might*) move up faster.

CORRECT: If she worked here, *maybe* she *could* move up faster.

PRACTICE 16-C
Correct this sentence three ways.

If we had left earlier, we might could have seen Tom.

THE AWKWARD REPETITION OF *HAD*

16:10   The following sentence is correct:

We would have driven to Quebec last year if we *had had* a reliable car.

The doubling of *had* is correct, but it looks and sounds awkward. The best way to improve the sentence is to replace the second *had* with another verb.

We would have driven to Quebec last year if we *had owned* a reliable car.

We would have driven to Quebec last year if we *had bought* a reliable car.

We would have driven to Quebec last year if our car *had been* reliable.

Here is another example:

CORRECT: If she *had had* more training, she could have asked for a raise.

BETTER: If she *had signed up* for more training, she could have asked for a raise.

BETTER: If she *had taken* more courses, she could have asked for a raise.

BETTER: If she *had been* trained in more areas, she could have asked for a raise.

PRACTICE 16-D
Reword these sentences to avoid doubling *had*.

1. He might have won the election if he had had a better campaign manager.

2. If we had had more money with us, we would have bought twice as much.

3. She couldn't have looked sillier if she had had a feather in her ear.

English for Professionals

EXERCISE 16
THE SUBJUNCTIVE

16:11   I. Correct or improve the following sentences by marking out the incorrect or awkward words and replacing them.

1. If they had had less help, they might not have finished on time.

2. If Trung had been with us, he would of done his share of the work.

3. If you would accept that job, you might could attend night school.

4. If Ernestine was in charge, we would not be working every weekend.

5. If the cabinet had had more compartments, we would have ordered it.

6. I wish I was in London where my sisters live.

7. He could of worked all day if you had asked him to.

8. I would have agreed to the contract if the company had had more effective accounting procedures.

9. If he qualifies for the position, he might could move to Hawaii.

10. Mark might of won the race if he had had better shoes.

16:12   II. Consider these statements false. Restate them in the subjunctive mood.

1. I am as strong as Superman. (Make a wish.)

   I wish I . . .

2. I am as strong as Superman, and I can leap tall buildings. (Use an *if-could* sentence.)

   If I . . .

3. You were there, and we played pinochle all day. (Use an *if-would* sentence.)

   If you . . .

4. Ramona is as busy now as she was last year. (Make a wish.)

   I wish Ramona . . .

5. Roy and Dale are here, and they will not let Snidely McWhiplash evict us. (Use an *if-would* sentence.)

   If Roy and Dale . . .

17 ACTIVE VOICE VERSUS PASSIVE VOICE

17:01 Understanding the difference between active voice and passive voice is one of the keys to avoiding pomposity. (See 18:19.) Study this chapter carefully.

ACTIVE VOICE

17:02 *Active voice* refers to sentences where the subject is the *DOER*, the person or thing that does whatever is being done. Here are two examples:

 John hit the ball through the window.

 The moon lit up the courtyard.

John, the subject of the first sentence, is the *DOER*. He is the person who acted to hit the ball. *The moon*, the subject of the second sentence, is also the *DOER*. It's the thing that acted to light up the courtyard.

When the subject of a sentence is the *DOER*, the sentence is in *active voice*.

PASSIVE VOICE

17:03 *Passive voice* refers to sentences where the subject of the sentence is the *DOEE*, the person or thing being acted upon by an outside force (the *DOER*). In *passive voice*, the subject of the sentence doesn't do anything. Instead, something happens to the subject while it remains *passive*. Examine these new versions of the previous two examples:

 The ball was hit through the window *by* John.

 The courtyard was lit up *by* the moon.

The ball, the subject of the first sentence, is the *DOEE*. It's the thing acted upon *by* John (the *DOER*). *The court yard*, the subject of the second sentence, is also a *DOEE*. It was lit up *by* the moon (the *DOER*).

When the subject of a sentence is the *DOEE*, the sentence is in *passive voice*.

Notice that in passive voice the *DOER*s (*John* and *the moon*) have been moved toward the back of their sentences and are tied to their sentences with the word *by*. With the *DOER*s, in the back of these sentences, we can take passive voice one step farther and drop the *DOER*s.

 The ball was hit through the window.

 The courtyard was lit up.

Passive voice states that something has been done. Sometimes it names the *DOER*, and sometimes it doesn't.

83

USING ACTIVE VOICE

17:04 Use active voice whenever the *DOER* plays a role in the sentence.

Active voice is our most common mode of expression. Why? Most of the time, we are concerned with who does what, and when we are, *active voice* is clearer and shorter.

Does that fact mean we should always avoid *passive voice*? No.

USING PASSIVE VOICE

17:05 Sometimes, passive voice is the better choice. Use it when the *DOER* does not need to be mentioned. Here are three typical cases:

1. Use passive voice when something was done, but we don't care or know who did it.

   Are you sure the lights have been turned off? Yes, they have been turned off. (We don't care who did it.)

   The elderly man next door has been robbed. (We don't know who did it.)

2. Use passive voice when a large, diverse group is the *DOER*. Here are two examples:

   Most steam locomotives have been relegated to museums or scrap heaps. (This sentence is better than "People have relegated most steam locomotives to museums or scrap heaps.")

   In New York, the arts are given the support they deserve. ("In New York, the community gives the arts the support they deserve" uses more words and is less effective.)

3. Use passive voice when the *DOER* is obvious.

   My leave request was approved. (Everyone knows the supervisor had to approve it.)

Use passive voice whenever the *DOER* might as well be left out of the sentence.

ABUSING PASSIVE VOICE

17:06 People who use passive voice when they should use active voice violate one principle of good style.

The easiest way to spot the abuse of passive voice is to search for the word *by*. When a *DOER* follows *by*, the sentence probably needs revision. Most of the time, such sentences should be changed to make the *DOER* the subject. Consider these two examples:

The letter will be mailed *by* 12 noon.

The article was written *by* an African diplomat.

The first example contains the word *by*, but *12 noon* is not a *DOER*. Since we probably don't know or care who will mail the letter, this sentence should be left as it is.

The second example also contains the word *by*, and this time a *DOER*, the *African diplomat*, follows it. The sentence should be rewritten to read, "An African diplomat wrote the article." It is now two words shorter and more direct.

English for Professionals

Chances are, "The article was written by an African diplomat" sounds all right to you. You must agree that the revised version is shorter and more direct, but you probably doubt that the small improvement justified the effort of revising the sentence.

You are correct. The occasional abuse of passive voice is scarcely worth noticing. Passive voice becomes a problem when someone abuses it again and again.

People who habitually abuse passive voice think it makes them appear intellectual. The abuse of passive voice is one of the hallmarks of gobbledygook.

Read the following passage (notice how the word *by* alerts you to the abuse of passive voice):

> An announcement has been issued *by* the president's office to the effect that an in-service will be held *by* the director of personnel for all department heads. The information presented *by* him will be used *by* the department heads to evaluate applications submitted *by* potential employees. (46 words)

17:07 It sounds fancy, doesn't it? Still, the *by*s tell us that the passage should be rewritten in active voice. Active voice will make the message clearer, shorter, and more effective (and will remove the *by*s).

> The president's office has issued an announcement to the effect that the director of personnel will hold an in-service for all department heads. The information he will present will help the department heads evaluate applications that potential employees submit. (39 words)

The *by*s are gone, the sentences are more straightforward, and the word count is 15 percent lower, but most readers sense that something is still wrong. The passage seems to use too many words. The beauty of active voice is that it begs for simplification.

> The president's office has announced that the director of personnel will hold an in-service for all department heads. His presentation will help the department heads evaluate employment applications. (28 words)

The most damning characteristic of passive voice is that it begs for complication. When passive voice is combined with clichés and jargon, it can waste countless hours and dollars. Can you understand this revision?

> An operational support announcement has been disseminated by the office of our company's chief executive officer to the effect that an interactive in-service will be convened by the director of corporate personnel. The information to be disseminated by the DoCP is designed to enhance the cognizant department head's performance in the evaluation of employment inquiries. (55 words)

Such nonsense should not impress professionals. Your job is to communicate. The most effective way to communicate is to be direct and precise. Use passive voice when it's appropriate, but don't abuse it. Never use passive voice to sound intellectual.

17:08   **EXERCISE 17**
ACTIVE VOICE VERSUS PASSIVE VOICE

I. The following sentences are in active voice. Convert them to passive voice.

1. Mary Carter gave a presentation on office layouts.

2. Our new printer turned out the report in record time.

3. Someone repaired our old printer.

4. Our old printer turns out better looking reports than the new one does.

5. The passengers, the press, and airport officials gave the crew credit for saving our lives.

Do any of these sentences work better in passive voice? Why?

17:09   II. The following sentences are in passive voice. Convert them to active voice.

1. A meeting for employees interested in college classes was scheduled by the director.

2. The report was written by Jane, and it will be edited by Wanda.

3. Our house has been painted.

4. The chair was delivered last Friday.

5. The Constitution was written in 1787.

Do any of these sentences work better in passive voice? Why?

17:10   III. Circle the *by*s in the following paragraph. Then, on a separate sheet of paper, translate it into active voice.

A bulletin has been prepared by the grievance committee concerning smoking by employees in the halls. Objections to the smoke are being raised by some nonsmokers. If a solution to the problem can't be found by the employees, all smoking could be outlawed by the president. Suggestions should be submitted by concerned employees so a compromise can be reached. (59 words)

How many words are in your revision? Is your version clearer?

Now that the paragraph is in active voice, can you simplify it further?

Should "so a compromise can be reached" be left in passive voice? Why?

18 THE BUSINESS STYLE: SIMPLE CLARITY

18:01 Most of us have been exposed to at least three distinct writing styles: the academic style, bureaucratic gobbledygook, and the business style.

If you attended a typical college, you took two semesters of composition where you wrote ten to fifteen essays and a research paper or two. You then took two semesters of literature and wrote papers about poems, short stories, and novels.

In these classes, your instructors required you to use the academic style. They probably never mentioned the principles of business writing. Unfortunately, English professors rarely discuss the business style, and if your college required you to take a course in business or technical writing, it was truly avant-garde.

The academic style is fine for colleges and universities. Its impersonal objectivity and its often obscure vocabulary serve a purpose. At its best, this style allows brilliant men and women to exchange complex ideas as they unlock the secrets of our universe, but the academic style was never intended for the business world.

The second style, bureaucratic gobbledygook, is a cheap imitation of the academic style and is often flavored with legal and technical jargon. If you have done battle with state or federal regulators, you have probably encountered bureaucratic gobbledygook. If you have never seen it, here it is.

> There is one matter of primal concern which must be conceptualized by any party in order to achieve cognizance in the realm of environment preservation strategies; that being, the fundamental right of one to possess a geographically delimited expanse of real estate entails no inherent privilege to willfully abuse or otherwise obfuscate the environmental support systems which are therein interdependent.

Such botched attempts to sound intellectual do little more than waste the reader's time. Why didn't the writer say "The right to own property does not carry with it the right to abuse our environment"?

Unfortunately, many business writers think they are expected to use the academic style, and others are convinced that bureaucratic gobbledygook is the mark of professionalism. These people are mistaken.

The style of business writing is the style of ***simple clarity***. Business writing should transfer information from the writer to the reader as efficiently as possible. Being a good business writer means avoiding some of the restraints of academic English and all the pomposity of bureaucratic gobbledygook.

AVOIDING THE RESTRAINTS OF ACADEMIC ENGLISH

18:02 1. Use first-person pronouns any time you need them.
In business writing, nothing is wrong with pronouns like *I, me, my, mine, myself, we, us, our, ours,* and *ourselves.*

>   POOR: *This office* would like to review the revised budget.

>   POOR: *The writer* would like to review the revised budget.

>   BETTER: *I* would like to review the revised budget.

Your English composition instructor was right. First-person pronouns are of questionable value in literary essays. In business writing, you need them for clarity.

18:03 2. Use second-person pronouns any time you need them.
Nothing is wrong with pronouns like *you, your, yours,* and *yourself* when we use them to address our readers. These pronouns are especially useful when we write instructions.

>   POOR: Additional information should be gathered on how to reduce the company's tax payments (written to the person who will do the work).

>   BETTER: Would *you* gather additional information on how the company can reduce its tax payments.

Your English composition instructor was right. You shouldn't use the pronoun *you* in literary essays. In business writing, however, using *you* can improve the tone and clarity of your letters, memorandums, and e-mails. It helps you focus your message on the reader. (See 20:04.)

18:04 3. Use short, simple sentences.
They are easier to understand, especially when your reader is in a hurry. An occasional long sentence will improve your sentence variety, and complex thoughts sometimes demand complex sentence structure, but don't let long, complex sentences dominate your written messages.

18:05 4. Use short paragraphs.
If you write a paragraph that is more than five lines long, look for a logical place to break it up. Like short sentences, short paragraphs are easier to read.

18:06 5. Use one-sentence paragraphs whenever your paragraphs need only one sentence.
Your composition instructor liked long, well-developed paragraphs and told you to avoid one-sentence paragraphs. In business writing, one-sentence paragraphs are common. They often help you emphasize important points.

18:07 Learning to write for business and industry means unlearning much of what your composition instructors taught you, but not because they were wrong. They were simply teaching you another style.

AVOIDING THE ERRORS OF POMPOSITY

18:08   1. Avoid professional jargon unless you are writing to a member of your profession.
Professional jargon can confuse people outside your profession.

>   POOR: Your boot drive has an inappropriate slot size adapter for the augmentation of the config.sys file.

>   BETTER: Your disk operating system is on the wrong diskette, so your computer won't work.

18:09   One type of professional jargon especially unfit for business writing is legal jargon. Legal jargon is for legal documents. (Lawyers might do well to minimize their use of it.)

>   POOR: The party desiring said equipment is currently sufficiently encumbered.

>   BETTER: The customer who ordered the tools has already reached his credit limit.

18:10   A popular example of legal jargon is *and/or*. (Some say it came from Boolean algebra.) Neither *and/or* nor other word combinations using diagonals are normally used in business writing.

Some people think jargon impresses readers. It's more likely to exasperate them.

18:11   2. Do not use the word *which* when *that* will do the job. (See 13:27.)

>   POOR: Have you seen the report *which* Joan wrote?

>   BETTER: Have you seen the report *that* Joan wrote?

>   STILL BETTER: Have you seen the report Joan wrote?

>   POOR: The letter in *which* you describe the problem is on my desk.

>   BETTER: Your letter describing the problem is on my desk.

Pompous writers seldom pass up a chance to use *which*.

18:12   NOTE: Many writers think they should use *which* to avoid ending a sentence with a preposition.

>   WEAK: I have found the job *of which* I have always dreamed.

>   BETTER: I have found the job I have always dreamed *of*.

No matter what you have been told, ending a sentence with a preposition is perfectly acceptable, unless the preposition is unnecessary.

>   CORRECT: Which contractor is she sending the specifications *to*?

>   INCORRECT: Where is Mr. Werthan *at*? (Drop the *at*.)

>   INCORRECT: *What* did she write that letter *for*? (*Why* did she write that letter?)

18:13   3. Avoid the word *shall*.
Shall is archaic (except when it's used in contracts and other documents to establish a legal obligation). Modern usage calls for *will*.

    POOR: We *shall* be happy to . . . .

    BETTER: We *will* be happy to . . . .

People who use *shall* usually hold the romantic notion that English has degenerated since the nineteenth century when *shall* was current.

18:14   4. Avoid noun piles.
When you use more than two nouns in a row, you create noun piles. ***Company memorandum format requirements*** and ***customer information file*** are noun piles. Break up noun piles by using prepositions like *to*, *of*, and *for*.

    POOR: Our ***employee training goals*** are part of our ***office efficiency improvement plan***.

    BETTER: Our ***goals <u>for</u> employee training*** are part ***<u>of</u>*** our ***plan <u>to</u> improve office efficiency***.

Pompous writers often take noun piles one painful step farther by placing an "impressive" but useless adjective in front of the noun pile.

    POOR: Our <u>***comprehensive***</u> ***employee training goals*** are part of our <u>***corporate***</u> ***office efficiency improvement plan***.

Americans borrowed noun piles from the German language. In German, noun piles occur naturally. English uses prepositions.

18:15   5. Don't dangle demonstrative pronouns (and avoid alliteration).
When you use the words *this*, *that*, *those*, *these*, and *such*, use them in front of nouns.

    POOR: *This* is interesting.

    BETTER: *This problem* is interesting.

    POOR: I enjoy reading articles *such as that*.

    BETTER: I enjoy reading *such* articles.

We dangle demonstrative pronouns when we speak because we can point as we speak.

    SPOKEN: *That* (pointing) will be Dean's.

    WRITTEN: *That office* will be Dean's.

When we write, we can't point, and we shouldn't dangle demonstrative pronouns.

An occasional dangling *that* or *this* will do no harm, but when you habitually dangle demonstrative pronouns, you shroud your sentences in pseudointellectual fog.

18:16   6. Don't misuse reflexive pronouns.
Never use reflexive pronouns (*myself, yourself, himself, herself, itself, ourselves, themselves,* and *oneself*) when another pronoun would be more natural.

>   POOR: The chancellor and *myself* reviewed your request.
>   (The chancellor reviewed it and myself reviewed it.)

>   BETTER: The chancellor and *I* reviewed your request.
>   (The chancellor reviewed it and I reviewed it.)

Public figures love to abuse *myself.* It's poor grammar, but they seem to think it's eloquent. For a more thorough explanation of this problem, see 2:05.

18:17   7. Never *feel badly* about anything.
Standard English allows us to *feel bad* about something, but when we *feel badly*, we are using the language *badly.* (See 13:09.)

18:18   8. Avoid the pronoun *one*.
The pronoun *one* is fairly common in academic circles, but it sounds archaic and stuffy to most business writers.

>   POOR: In Seattle, *one* must always keep *one's* umbrella handy.

>   BETTER: In Seattle, most people keep an umbrella handy.

The pronoun *one* can build a wall of formality between you and your reader.

18:19   9. Write in *active voice* unless you have a specific reason for using *passive voice*.

>   POOR: A seminar on benefits has been organized by the personnel director.

>   BETTER: The personnel director has organized a seminar on benefits.

Active voice is our normal mode of expression, and most of the time, it's clearer and shorter than passive voice. (For a thorough discussion of this topic, see Chapter 17.)

10. Avoid recipe English.
18:20   Recipe English is a type of shorthand sometimes seen in second-rate cookbooks and instruction manuals. It looks like this:

>   First, insert screwdriver into slot. Turn clockwise until tight.

It should read like this:

>   First, insert the screwdriver into the slot. Turn it clockwise until the screw is tight.

Recipe English drops most articles, prepositions, and conjunctions in an effort to save space. The price of this saved space can be high.

>   1. Recipe English saves time for the writer, but it wastes the reader's time, a violation of one of the basic principles of good writing.

>   2. Recipe English sacrifices clarity. This lack of clarity often costs money and can be dangerous.

Recipe English is poor style. Use full-blown sentences. Write as though you were talking to your parents over a cup of coffee.

11. Use plain English.

18:21 Use common words as they are commonly used.

> POOR: It is our intent that those supplemental monies abrogate his proclivity toward indolence.
>
> BETTER: We hope the raise will encourage him to work harder.

18:22 Pompous writers love to use uncommon verbs built from common nouns.

> have an *impact* on ➞ *to impact* (*To affect* is better.)
> to present *evidence* ➞ *to evidence* (*To prove* or *to demonstrate* is better.)
> a s*equence* of events ➞ *to sequence* (*To arrange* is better.)
>
> POOR: The way she **sequenced** the sessions **positively impacted** our ability to attend them and **evidenced** her respect for entry-level employees.
>
> BETTER: The way she **arranged** the sessions **allowed us to** attend them all and **demonstrated** her respect for entry-level employees.

18:23 Pompous writers also love to use uncommon plurals.

> *person* ➞ *persons* (*People* is better.)
> *money* ➞ *monies* (*Money* needs no plural.)
> *counseling* ➞ *counselings* (*Counseling sessions* is better.)
>
> POOR: After several **counselings**, we persuaded her to invest more **monies** in training for underqualified **persons**.
>
> BETTER: After several **counseling sessions**, we persuaded her to invest more **money** (or **funds**) in training for underqualified **people**.

Plain English is hardworking and honest.

18:24 When people fall victim to pomposity, they write to impress, not to inform. Remember, as a business writer, your job is to inform, not to impress. If you use clear, informative prose, you will win your reader's respect.

ADDITIONAL SUGGESTIONS

18:25 1. Don't ask the reader to read your mind.
Say exactly what you want to say, and say it as clearly as you can.

> POOR: Although she is a new employee, the supervisor wants Mary to work weekends.

Is Mary or the supervisor the new employee?

> BETTER: Although Mary is a new employee, her supervisor wants her to work weekends.

Such problems are the result of inexperience and carelessness. Think carefully about what you intend to say. After you have expressed yourself as clearly as you can, ask another person to check your writing for clarity. (See Chapter 22, "Proofreading Skills.")

18:26   2. Write short letters, memorandums, and e-mails.

One-page messages are best and two-page messages are acceptable, but something is usually wrong if a your letter, memorandum or e-mail exceeds two pages. If your message is more than one page long, ask yourself these questions:

    A. Have I been reasonably concise?
    B. Does all this information belong in the letter (instead of in an attachment)?
    C. Will this letter be more effective than a meeting or a telephone conversation?

If the answer to all three questions is *YES*, send the message.

18:27   3. Cull ~~out all~~ unnecessary words.

Using too many words dilutes your message.

    POOR: It was Juan who first thought of it.

    BETTER: Juan thought of it first.

4. Use good sentence variety.

18:28   Vary the length of your sentences.

Short sentences are better than long ones, but a solid block of short sentences often looks childish. Mix a few long sentences with your short sentences. Too many long sentences slow the reader down and might even seem pompous.

18:29   Vary the structure of your sentences. Use commas (correctly).

An ordinary sentence consists of a single independent clause with the subject in position one and the verb in position two. The remaining information then follows the verb. Because commas signal a departure from this ordinary structure, an easy way to ensure good sentence variety is to use commas.

Consider using at least two or three commas in every letter, memorandum or e-mail. (See Chapter 3.)

5. Use good word variety.

18:30   In every message, certain words are especially important. In a letter about the budget, such key words as ***budget***, ***expenses***, and ***requisitions*** may appear frequently. Use these key words as often as you need them. Do not use other substantial words more than once on a page (unless you repeat them for emphasis).

Words used too frequently lose their strength.

    POOR: Check with him again to see whether he can check the program for an error again.

    BETTER: Call him back and ask him to double-check the program for an error.

18:31   Clichés are words and phrases that were worn out before they reached you. You violate the principles of good style when you use them even once.

    POOR: In reference to your letter of September 12, permit me to say that, at the present time, the item you requested is temporarily out of stock.

    BETTER: The printer you ordered on September 12 is temporarily out of stock.

Some people think clichés add eloquence. They don't. Clichés are for parrots.

18:32 Redundancies are words and phrases that needlessly echo something. ***The reason why*** is probably our most popular redundancy. Here are some more:

> but yet (one or the other, not both)
> throughout the entire (***Throughout*** is enough.)
> a total of 95 people (95 people)
> the basic fundamentals (***The fundamentals*** is enough.)
> any afternoon after 4 PM (Drop the ***PM.***)

18:33 One of our most common redundancies usually goes unrecognized. When ***then*** follows an introductory element (comma Rule Two) that starts with ***when*** or ***if***, ***then*** is redundant.

> POOR: ***When*** (or ***If***) the new equipment comes in, ***then*** we can start construction.

> BETTER: ***When*** (or ***If***) the new equipment comes in, we can start construction.

18:34 The worst redundancies are double negatives (***don't never, won't never, can't hardly***). Using double negatives, like using ***ain't***, could mark you as an uneducated person.

Redundancies add words without adding content.

18:35 Another way to improve your word variety is to avoid the words ***real(ly), very,*** and ***get.*** (See 13:25 for a discussion of these threadbare words.)

18:36   6. Give your letters, memorandums, and e-mails enough ***white space.***
White space is the part of your page not covered with print. Think of white space as the part of your message that lets your reader breathe.

Crowded margins, long paragraphs, and WRITING WITH UPPERCASE LETTERS will devour your white space. Consider using 1.5-inch margins and limiting most of your paragraphs to five lines. Use uppercase letters sparingly. Also, ragged right margins seem to improve white space.

If your message has plenty of white space, the person you send it to will be more likely to read it, will read it faster, and will remember the message longer.

18:37 CALCULATING THE GRADE LEVEL OF YOUR WRITING

Over the years, reading specialists have devised ways to calculate the *reading level* of written materials. (Material with a reading level of 9 is on the ninth-grade level, a reading level of 13 is appropriate for college freshmen, etc.)

One easy way to calculate reading levels is to use **Gunning's FOG INDEX**, described in Robert Gunning's *The Technique of Clear Writing* (McGraw-Hill, 1968). To calculate the reading level of your writing, follow these steps. (Run the test on three examples of your writing and average the results.)

STEP 1: Select a sample of your writing that is about 100 words long, and count the words. Count every word. Hyphenated words count as a single word.

STEP 2: Count the sentences. If a sentence has two independent clauses (separated by a Rule One comma [3:02-06]), count it as two sentences.

STEP 3: Calculate the average number of words per sentence.

STEP 4: Count the number of difficult words (words with three or more syllables). Don't count proper nouns (*Chicago*). Don't count combinations of easy words (*housewarming, paperwork*). Don't count words that earn their third syllable by adding commonly used suffixes or prefixes like *-ing* (*believing*), *-es* (*processes*), or *un* (*unworthy*).

STEP 5: Calculate the percentage of difficult words (divide the number of difficult words by the total number of words, and multiply the result by 100).

STEP 6: Calculate the FOG INDEX (add the percent of difficult words to the average sentence length, and multiply that total by 0.4).

EXAMPLE (from the introduction to this book)

Hundreds of years ago, a single human being could know everything worth knowing. This ideal Renaissance man or woman studied medicine, law, philosophy, and the arts, often excelling in each field. Alas, such simple times have passed.

We are now immersed in a revolution. Technological advances and the unshackled creativity of democratic societies have given birth to a new era, the information age. No one alive would dare lay claim to all knowledge worth knowing.

Today, most of us specialize. We dedicate years of learning and productivity to a single field. Air travel, computer programming, banking, and countless other activities are made possible by scores of specialists, each doing what few others know how to do.

1. Number of words = 120
2. Number of sentences = 9
3. Average sentence length = 13.3
4. Number of difficult words (underlined) = 11
5. Percentage of difficult words = 9.2
6. 13.3 + 9.2 = 22.5,   22.5 X 0.4 = 9.0. (The Fog Index is ninth grade.)

The reading level of most newspapers is 8 or 9. Popular magazines may be a bit more difficult, 10 or 11. As shown by the example presented here, the average reading level of *CommonSense Grammar and Style* is somewhere around 9. Only academic writing routinely climbs above 12.

Try to keep the reading level of your business writing well below 12.

18:38 **TOPICS FOR DISCUSSION**

1. Did your high school and college English courses prepare you to write for the business world? Should you have been required to study the business style?

2. Why is someone from the private sector less likely to write bureaucratic gobbledygook?

3. Have you ever known anyone who could write clear, simple prose but still had a flair for creative writing? Would that style be suitable for business letters?

4. If first-person pronouns (*I, me, mine, my,* and *myself*) can be used in business correspondence, can they be overused? Explain.

5. The next time you attend a meeting where you can take notes without attracting attention, count the number of times you hear the words *real(ly), very*, and *get*. How often are these words used? What can be said about people who rarely use them?

6. Most people avoid books with small print and narrow margins. Why?

7. Examine a textbook, an article, or a reference work that a leading professional in your field has written. Can you find passages lacking clarity? Suggest ways to improve the clarity.

8. Read over something you wrote several months or years ago. What is the reading level? Is it clear? Can you improve it by applying the guidelines in this chapter?

18:39 **EXERCISE 18**
CLARITY
Analyze the following sentences.
A. How do they violate the principles of simple clarity?
B. Repair each sentence.

1. According to Ms. Howard's instructions, we should set up a meeting with the contractors to convince them that they should let us occupy the new building before the parking lot and/or the landscaping is complete, and if they agree, we need to work out a plan for the move.

    A.

    B.

2. Mr. Van Buren and myself will be in charge of the corporate vehicles inspection procedures.

    A.

    B.

3. My physician said that I am suffering from pharyngitis with rhinorrhea, so my physician prescribed ASA and bed rest.

    A.

    B.

4. A very important decision has been reached by the president concerning the annual bonuses paid by the company.

   A.

   B.

5. Open valve in line feeding pump. Turn on.

   A.

   B.

6. Yours truly shall be at your office by midafternoon.

   A.

   B.

7. The report should be completed/distributed by the end of the month. (This request is aimed at the person who is supposed to do the job.

   A.

   B.

8. If one gets the opportunity, then one should invest one's money in high-yield bonds.

   A.

   B.

9. As your factory representative, the author of this letter is deeply committed to servicing the customer.

   A.

   B.

10. Before selecting the desired option from the main menu, a password should be keyed in, and *ENTER* should be pressed. (This passage comes from software instructions.)

   A.

   B.

11. Senator Fogbound felt badly about the mistake and extended a really heartfelt apology to William and myself.

   A.

   B.

12. The reason why she came is because she wanted to see Mike.

   A.

   B.

13. The passwords upon which our users will rely to access the mainframe must be assigned today. (The person reading this message is the one who will assign the passwords.)

   A.

   B.

14. This is only designed to burn diesel fuel.

   A.

   B.

15. Enclosed please find the résumé which you so kindly requested. If you would care to review my references or make further inquiry pertaining to my professional credentials, I shall get them to you without further delay.

   A.

   B.

19 EMPHASIZING IMPORTANT INFORMATION

19:01 Have you ever read and reread a letter, struggling to determine what it's all about? Have you ever written a letter requesting information or permission to do something only to receive a response that missed the mark? Unfortunately, many people face similar problems.

Knowing how to emphasize specific words, phrases, and ideas will help you make your main points stand out. Knowing how to emphasize important information means less writing.

This chapter presents eight formal and four less formal ways to emphasize information.

FORMAL METHODS OF EMPHASIS (FOR LETTERS, MEMORANDUMS, AND E-MAILS)

19:02 1. Say something is important. Then say why it's important.

> It's extremely important that you complete the roof by the 15th of November. If winter rains saturate the interior cement structures, further construction could be delayed by weeks.

19:03 2. State the important information at the appropriate place in the letter. Then repeat it at the end of the letter.

> In closing, I must reiterate that all work will come to a halt if your drawings are not in our hands by June 1.

These first two methods are forceful. If you find them too forceful, try one of the following approaches.

19:04 3. Place the important information at the beginning or at the end of the letter. The outline for good- and neutral-news letters (20:02) follows this guideline.

19:05 4. Place the important information in short, simple sentences.

> Please print. Use one block for each letter.

19:06 5. Place the important information in a one-sentence paragraph. This method surrounds the information with white space and helps it catch the reader's eye. (See 18:36.)

19:07 6. Use specific language to state the important information.

> You completed the project 43 days ahead of schedule and spent $2.3 million less than we had projected.

19:08   7. When you want to stress three or more points or ask three or more questions, arrange them in a column. To give the points additional emphasis, number them, letter them, or set them off with bullets.

If you use a typewriter, follow these steps to make bullets:
- Type a lowercase *o*.
- Single-space.
- Type the information.
- Fill in the *o* with a black pen.

19:09   8. Indent the block of information that needs to be emphasized. Indented blocks are used to make the examples in this book stand out.

Indenting an entire paragraph is useful when the information that needs emphasis is long and complicated.

19:10   **INFORMAL METHODS OF EMPHASIS (FOR MEMORANDUMS AND E-MAILS)**
1. <u>Underline</u> important information.

2. Use **bold** letters to present important information.

3. Write important information in CAPITAL LETTERS.

4. If you are sending only a few copies, mark over the important information with a felt-tipped highlighter.

19:11   **DE-EMPHASIZING INFORMATION**
Sometimes, information deserves to be de-emphasized, especially when the reader will find it unpleasant.

The easiest and best way to de-emphasize something is simple. Don't mention it.

The next-best way is to refrain from emphasizing it. Use general language, place the information in a long, complex sentence, or bury it in the middle of a long paragraph. The indirect approach to bad-news messages (20:11-21) uses these methods.

19:12   **TOPICS FOR DISCUSSION**
1. What happens when a writer emphasizes too many points?

2. Can you think of situations that might require you to emphasize unpleasant information?

3. What other methods have you used for emphasizing important information?

4. Can you think of other ways to de-emphasize negative information?

5. When might you use the informal methods of emphasis in letters?

English for Professionals

EXERCISE 19
EMPHASIS
Examine the following pairs. Which one places the strongest emphasis on the underlined phrase? What methods of emphasis are used?

1. The deadline is midnight, April 15.

    A. The envelope must be postmarked no later than midnight, April 15.

    B. The envelope must be postmarked **no later than midnight, April 15**.

2. The order needs to be placed immediately.

    A. I suggest that you go ahead and place your order today.

    B. Order now. Don't wait.

3. This letter is riddled with errors.

    A. I think you forgot to proofread this letter.

    B. Look at this letter. You misspelled five words and left out seven commas.

4. Motivation is more effective than intimidation.

    A. If her presentation had one central idea, it was the importance of motivation.

    Supervisors must learn that motivated employees are more efficient than intimidated employees.

    B. If her presentation had one central idea, it was that supervisors should try to motivate their employees, not intimidate them.

5. All drivers must be tested for drugs.

    A. By the end of the week, all drivers must be tested for drugs.

    B. By the end of the week, ALL DRIVERS must be tested for drugs.

6. Payment is due within ten days.

    A. You must send us <u>a check for $350</u>, and it must reach us <u>within ten days</u>.

    B. You must send us a check for $350, and it must reach us within ten days.

7. <u>The telephone, the computer, and the copier need to be repaired.</u>

   A. The following items in our office need to be repaired: the telephone, the computer, and the copier.

   B. In our office, the following items need to be repaired:
      - The telephone
      - The computer
      - The copier

8. <u>The computer needs to be repaired first.</u>

   A. It's important that the computer be repaired first because we have to complete about 20 bid requests this week.

   B. We would like you to have the computer repaired first.

9. <u>A meeting will be held Monday, July 18, at 9:30 AM.</u>

   A. Representatives from our major contractors will be here next week. I want each of you to give them a tour of your area, and I want you to explain your role in the project. On Monday, July 18, at 9:30 AM, we will meet to lay the groundwork for the week's activities. If you have any questions about the project, we will discuss them at the meeting. I look forward to seeing you there.

   B. Representatives of each of the major contractors will be here next week. I want each of you to give them a tour of your area, and I want you to explain your role in the project.

   On Monday, July 18, at 9:30 AM, we will meet to lay the groundwork for the week's activities.

   If you have any questions about the project, we will discuss them at the meeting. I look forward to seeing you there.

10. <u>A meeting will be held Monday, July 18, at 9:30 AM.</u>

    A. On Monday, July 18, at 9:30 AM, we will meet to lay the groundwork for the week's activities. Representatives of each of the major contractors will be there. I want each of you to give them a tour of your area, and I want you to explain your role in the project.

    If you have any questions about the project, we will discuss them at the meeting. I look forward to seeing you there.

    B. Representatives of each of the major contractors will be here next week. On Monday, July 18, at 9:30 AM, we will meet to lay the groundwork for the week's activities. I want each of you to give them a tour of your area, and I want you to explain your role in the project.

    If you have any questions about the project, we will discuss them at the meeting. I look forward to seeing you there.

20 ORGANIZING LETTERS

20:01 Most writing in business and industry takes the form of letters, memorandums, or e-mails. These letters and memorandums perform a variety of tasks. Occasionally, they are simple acts of courtesy, as in a letter of congratulations, but most of the time, they transfer important information from the writer to the reader. They carry a message.

The difference between a well-written message and a poorly written message depends largely on how well you, the writer, anticipate your reader's reaction. In writing, as in conversation, some situations permit a straightforward approach while others demand tact.

The first part of this chapter discusses the straightforward or *direct approach*, and the second part deals with the tactful or *indirect approach*. The direct approach is used to convey news that will please (or at least not displease) the reader. The indirect approach is used, in most instances, to present information the reader will find unpleasant.

ORGANIZING GOOD- AND NEUTRAL-NEWS MESSAGES

20:02 Letters, memorandums, and e-mails that please the reader or provide routine information are the easiest to write. They make routine announcements, grant requests, confirm the shipment of orders, and otherwise promote a cooperative atmosphere. Keep these messages simple.

The typical good- or neutral-news message has three or more paragraphs. The first paragraph presents the news, the middle paragraph (or paragraphs) provides any necessary details, and the final paragraph closes on a positive note. Here is an outline of this approach.

THE DIRECT APPROACH

STEP 1: State the main point.

STEP 2: Provide details and explanations.

STEP 3: Close on a pleasant or forward-looking note, or display a positive attitude.

If no explanations or details are necessary, you can omit STEP 2. If your explanations and details are complex, STEP 2 can be divided into several paragraphs.

20:03 When you write good- or neutral-news messages, be polite. Use positive language, even when the information is bland.

20:04 One simple way to improve the tone of your messages is to make them *you-oriented*. A *you-oriented* message uses the word *you* often. The frequent use of *you* is not a cynical attempt to flatter the reader. It simply helps you focus on your reader, which is exactly what you should do.

20:05 When you close good- or neutral-news messages, be pleasant, but avoid clichés like "Have a nice day" or "Please accept my kindest regards."

20:06 NOTE: At times, you might study a request carefully before deciding to write a positive or good-news response. Once you commit yourself to a positive response, follow through. Don't let your good-news messages betray a begrudging or hesitant attitude.

The following letter uses the direct approach to convey good news.

20:07   1. Background: The owner of a small-engine repair shop has ordered several parts for a recently introduced garden tiller. He also wants to open an account so he can continue ordering parts as he needs them and pay at the end of each month. His credit record is impeccable. This letter comes from the supplier.

Paragraph 1
(STEP 1: State the main point.) *We shipped the parts for the Fuji Model 350 tiller today and charged them to your new account.*

Paragraph 2a
(STEP 2: Provide details and explanations.) *Your statement for this order and all future orders will arrive around the 1st of the month, and payment is due by the 15th. You will earn a 3 percent discount if your payment reaches us before the 10th.*

Paragraph 2b
(STEP 2 is continued.) *The drive chain we shipped you is several centimeters longer than the one you requested. Your chain is temporarily out of stock, but the one we sent is easy to shorten, and you can save the extra links for repairs.*

Paragraph 3
(STEP 3: Close on a positive or forward-looking note.) *We have enclosed several new order forms and an updated listing of our parts inventory. Thank you for placing your order with Alexander's Machine Supply.*

20:08   NOTE: This letter ends by saying *thank you*. The *thank you* is logical because it refers to something that has been done. Don't thank someone for something not yet done. You might say "I will appreciate . . ." or "I look forward to . . . ," but don't use *thoughtless thank you*s. They sound hollow.

Here is a memorandum that uses the direct approach to convey neutral news.

20:09   2. Background: The monthly business meeting has been scheduled, and the administrative assistant is sending out the announcements.

Paragraph 1
(STEP 1: State the main point.) *This month, we will hold our business meeting in Conference Room II on Thursday, October 24, at 1:30 PM.*

Paragraph 2
(STEP 2: Provide details and explanations.) *Bill Lawlor will report on the construction of our new office building. We also want to open discussions that will involve you in the selection of a new mainframe computer.*

Paragraph 3
(STEP 3: Close on a positive or forward-looking note.) *Please arrange your schedules so you can attend. I look forward to seeing you there.*

20:10   Good- and neutral-news messages are easy to write. The opening states the central idea, the middle, when needed, provides the details, and the closing adds a positive or forward-looking note. The sentences are short and uncluttered and display a positive attitude.

ORGANIZING BAD-NEWS MESSAGES

20:11　Bad-news letters, memorandums, and e-mails deny requests and otherwise refuse to cooperate because something is wrong. They are the most difficult messages to write.

In unpleasant situations, people often react emotionally. Frustration, disappointment, and anger can come into play and can do more harm than the bad news itself. The ability to present bad news properly is an important skill. People who don't know how to say *NO* frequently find themselves in trouble.

20:12　The most important difference between good-news and bad-news messages is that good-news messages open with the main point. Bad-news messages usually explain first. Then they present the main point (the bad news). This opening explanation displays the writer's respect for the reader.

The typical bad-news message has three paragraphs. The first paragraph opens on a courteous or positive note. The second explains, says *NO*, and ends on a positive note. The closing paragraph is also positive, making the final effort to maintain the reader's goodwill. Here is a detailed outline.

THE INDIRECT APPROACH
Paragraph 1:
Open with a neutral or positive statement related to the topic.

20:13　Do not state the obvious (I received your letter) or hint that a *YES* is coming. (We were pleased to receive your order.)

Paragraph 2:
Explain.

20:14　When you present your reasons for saying *NO*, use general language to de-emphasize them. Be honest and as brief as possible. The reader deserves an honest explanation but will skip down the page if it's long-winded.

Say *NO* gracefully.

20:15　To say *NO* gracefully, consider these suggestions.
　A.　Avoid negative words (*no, cannot, however, regret, but, unfortunately*, etc).
　　　A good way to avoid negative words and establish a more positive tone is to concentrate on what can be done, not what can't be done.

　B.　Avoid first-person singular pronouns (*I, me, my, mine*). Instead, use the plural forms (*we, us, our*). If you use plural pronouns, the refusal will sound less personal.

　C.　Bury the refusal in a long, complex sentence that is part of a three- to five-sentence paragraph. Burying the refusal de-emphasizes it.

End on a positive note.

20:16　Ending this middle paragraph on a positive note is important. Ending it with the refusal would emphasize the refusal. (See 19:04.)

Paragraph 3
Close on another positive note.

20:17　Try one or both of the following tactics:
　A.　Offer an alternative.
　　　If you deny credit, mention the layaway plan. If you refuse a request for a favor, suggest some other course of action. Look for another way to serve the reader.

　B.　Refer confidently to future business relations.
　　　If you deny credit, mention discounts or upcoming sales to encourage the reader to continue doing business on a cash basis. If you refuse a request for a favor, refer to future circumstances that might cause you to reconsider.

Here are four additional guidelines to help you deal tactfully with bad news.

20:18   1. As with good- or neutral-news messages, bad-news messages should be *you-oriented*. (See 20:04.)

20:19   2. Do not apologize for saying *NO* unless you are at fault and your reader deserves an apology. If you explain, you need not apologize.

20:20   3. Do not pass the buck. Don't blame the refusal on another person or on company policy. No professional would ever say "Look buddy, I just work here." If the refusal originates with another person, give that person's reasons. If it stems from company policy, explain the reasoning behind the policy.

20:21   4. Do not lecture the reader. Don't tell the reader something that is common knowledge. Anytime you could add the phrase "Now *YOU* know . . . ." in front of your statement, you are probably lecturing. Lectures are as insulting to adults as they are to children.

The following letter uses the indirect approach to present bad news. It follows the outline and respects the four additional guidelines for writing a bad-news message.

20:22   1. Background: The writer works for an orphanage. The president of a civic organization, Mr. Conners, has asked her to show a slide presentation that she developed, at her own expense, around her recent tour of Korean orphanages. For her talk, and a 300-mile round trip, he promises her a free meal, nothing else. She feels slighted, but her response takes the proper approach.

Paragraph 1
(STEP 1: Open with a neutral or positive statement related to the topic.) *I am always pleased to hear from people who share my concern for orphans.*

Paragraph 2
(STEP 2: Explain.) *Koreans and Americans live on opposite sides of the earth, but our problems are similar, and we have much to learn from one another. As with our Korean friends, rising costs require us to control expenditures and to concentrate on activities of direct benefit to the children we serve.* (STEP 3: Say *NO* gracefully.) *As enjoyable as the trip to Irvington would be, restrictions on travel keep us close to home.* (STEP 4: End this paragraph on a positive note.) *Our children's needs are great, but with the support of civic groups like yours, they can look forward to a happier and more productive future.*

Paragraph 3
(STEP 5: Close on another positive note.) *Mr. Conners, you and the other members of your organization can still see my entire slide presentation. On the last Sunday of this month, WHB-TV will air a telethon to raise money for Korean and American orphanages. The show will be built around my slides.*

Mr. Conners' request was insensitive (unless, perhaps, he planned to surprise her with a large donation), but her response was rational and respectful, and notice how well she said *NO* without using negative words. Instead of scolding, she took a sound, businesslike approach, one that could bring in a generous check.

English for Professionals

The next example is a letter more typical of business writing.

20:23   2. Background: The writer is the credit manager for a wholesale furniture warehouse. A local dealer, Ms. Wilson, has ordered three expensive bedroom suites and wants to buy them on credit. A check of her credit rating shows that she is seriously behind in her payments to another wholesaler.

Paragraph 1
(STEP 1: Open with a neutral or positive statement related to the topic.) *Your interest in the Williamsburg Regal bedroom suites is understandable. They are the finest factory reproductions we've seen in years.*

Paragraph 2
(STEP 2: Explain.) *A routine review of your credit references suggested that you are having difficulty meeting your current obligations and that a direct purchase would be in your best interest and ours.* (STEP 3: Say *NO* gracefully.) *We suggest that you order a single bedroom suite and pay for it on delivery. When you sell the first suite, you can order a second.* (STEP 4: End this paragraph on a positive note.) *We will be happy to review your credit application when your financial position improves.*

Paragraph 3
(STEP 5: Close on another positive note.) *I am enclosing a brochure listing Williamsburg Regal's complete line of reproductions. When you drop by, a member of our sales staff will show you the samples and take your order.*

Admittedly, Ms. Wilson might not be able to pay cash for an expensive bedroom suite. Still, this response treats her with respect and deals with her honestly. If her business improves, she will be back.

THE DIRECT APPROACH TO BAD NEWS

20:24   Most of the time, you should use the indirect approach to say *NO*. In the following situations, however, you should follow the direct approach (say *NO* first, explain, and then try to end on a pleasant note).

1. When an emergency exists and diplomacy would take too much time. Here, you probably would drop the explanation altogether.

2. When you and your reader know each other well and have already established mutual respect. In such cases, the indirect approach would be unnecessarily delicate and might leave your friend puzzled.

3. When the reader fails to understand the indirect approach or becomes insistent.

4. When the reader knowingly asks you to do something unethical or illegal.

20:25   Here is the letter Ms. Wilson (the furniture dealer who was denied credit [20:23]) received after she ignored the first, indirect *NO* and ordered the three bedroom suites on credit.

Paragraph 1
(STEP 1: State the main point.) *We sincerely regret that we cannot fill your order for the three Williamsburg Regal bedroom suites.*

Paragraph 2

(**STEP 2: Provide details and explanations.**) *Your credit record indicates that you are having trouble meeting other financial obligations. New credit purchases could incur risks neither of us wants to face.*

Paragraph 3

(**STEP 3: Close on a positive or forward-looking note.**) *We remain eager to serve you if you are willing to pay on delivery, and we will happily review your request for credit once your accounts are up to date.*

20:26   The approach is direct, even blunt, but the letter is courteous. Every rule in business writing has its exceptions, every rule but one: *NEVER BE RUDE.*

20:27 **TOPICS FOR DISCUSSION**

1. Can the guidelines for writing good- or neutral-news messages be applied to spoken messages?

2. Can the guidelines for writing bad-news messages be applied to spoken messages?

3. "At times, you might study a request carefully before deciding to write a positive or good-news response. Once you commit yourself to a positive response, follow through. Don't let your good-news messages betray a begrudging or hesitant attitude." Can you think of exceptions to this rule?

4. The standard approach to good- or neutral-news messages calls for a positive or forward-looking conclusion. Can you think of times when such a conclusion might be a waste of the writer's and the reader's time?

5. Some people think the positive or forward-looking conclusion is useless in good- and neutral-news memos sent to friends. Do you agree?

6. Why are memorandums that say *NO* more likely to use the direct approach than are letters that say *NO*?

7. In Chapter 18, "The Business Style: Simple Clarity," you were encouraged to use short paragraphs (18:05). When, according to Chapter 20, "Organizing Letters," is that advice wrong?

8. Good- or neutral-news messages commonly take the direct approach. Can you think of instances when good or neutral news might profit from the indirect approach?

9. How would you react if a close friend asked you for a favor and, in doing so, knowingly asked you to do something illegal or unethical?

10. You have been given four situations that justify the direct approach to bad news. Can you think of others?

11. Have you ever received an insulting letter? How did you react? How should you have reacted?

12. Why are rude or insensitive messages more likely to come from government bureaucracies than from private enterprise?

13. What circumstances might justify an insulting letter?

20:28 **EXERCISE 20**
LETTERS

1. One of your employees submits a written request for permission to enroll in a computer course at a local college.

   To attend, he must take a two-hour lunch break three times a week for eight weeks. You like the idea. His new skills will have immediate application to your division's activities, and the lost time is no problem. He always meets his responsibilities without so much as casting an eye at the clock.

   Write a memorandum saying *YES*, and remind him that the company will pay for the course if he makes a *C* or better. Personnel has the forms he needs.

2. You work for an accounting firm. One of your clients, a wealthy widow, requests a complete statement of her assets and liabilities so she can meet with representatives of an investment firm and plan some long-term investments for her grandchildren.

   Respond by letter. Tell her a partial statement will reach her within ten days, but certain information on property taxes will not be available for three or four weeks since the county is reassessing property values. You will send those data as soon as possible.

3. Find a good- or neutral-news letter you wrote before you studied this chapter. Critique it using the principles taught here.

4. One of your employees submits a written request for permission to enroll in a computer course at a local college.

   To attend, he must take a two-hour lunch break three times a week for eight weeks. You don't like the idea. The course has no application to your division's activities, and the lost time will create serious problems since his team is already behind on a major project. To make matters worse, his job performance has not been all you hoped for.

   You feel compelled to say *NO*. Write the memorandum.

5. You work for an accounting firm. Bob, a local real estate agent (the same one who recently helped you and your spouse buy your dream home at an exceptionally low price), asks for your help.

   Bob wants to make an offer on an office building that one of your clients owns. Rumor has it that the client is experiencing a cash flow problem. If Bob can confirm those rumors, he can approach the negotiations from a position of strength. All Bob asks is that you check the records and give him a sign.

   Respond by writing Bob a letter.

6. Find a bad-news letter you wrote before you studied this chapter. Critique it using the principles taught here.

21 SPECIAL LETTERS

21:01   The direct and indirect approaches to business messages can be applied to most writing situations, but certain letters, memorandums, and e-mails require a special approach.

These messages are unique because they don't say *YES*, they don't say *NO*, and they don't even carry routine news. Employment applications (résumé cover letters), interview follow-up notes, recommendations, resignations, dismissals, congratulatory notes, and thank-you notes are all special messages.

The guidelines in this chapter show how you can structure each of these special messages.

1. EMPLOYMENT APPLICATIONS (RÉSUMÉ COVER LETTERS)

21:02   Include the following points in a letter of application (to be mailed as the cover letter for a well-written résumé).

1. Name the position you now hold (a graduating student, an experienced professional, or another position). If the signature block of the letter (or the heading of the memorandum) names that position, don't repeat it in the body.

2. Ask for an interview (not for a job), and name the specific position that interests you. Mention any limitations on the times you can appear for the interview, or if your schedule is flexible, say you can come for an interview at the employer's convenience.

3. Say how you learned of the opening. You might mention a newspaper ad, a friend, an employment office, or some other source. The employer will be more comfortable if you give your point of origin.

4. Mention the one or two points from your résumé that best qualify you for this specific position. (If the job has been advertised, make sure they match the qualifications called for in the ad.) Keep this portion of the message short. Too many people belabor their qualifications in the application message when their résumé presents the same information. All you want to do in your letter is highlight the most important details.

5. Say something mildly pleasant. A pleasant closing ends your letter on a positive note and sets a positive tone for the upcoming interview.

6. Mention your résumé in the last sentence of your letter, not before. It may be even better to allow the word *résumé* to fall at the end of the last sentence. That word will encourage your reader to turn immediately to your résumé.

21:03   IMPORTANT NOTE: Arrange the first four points in any order that suits you. Point five should be the next-to-last item in the letter, and point six should be the last.

21:04   The following example uses this format.

> As a recent graduate of Twin Cities' electronics program and as an experienced salesman, I am interested in electronics sales.
>
> Your advertisement in *The Record* for an agent to market computer hardware caught my attention. Could we arrange an interview to discuss the position? I can meet any day before 2 PM.

> In addition to my training in electronics and sales, I have extensive experience with the microcomputers your company manufactures. We used them in our labs at college, and I worked with your Model RG-V when I lived in St Louis. Your products have earned my respect, and I could represent your company with pride.
>
> I hope to hear from you soon. My address and telephone number are on the attached résumé.

21:05 In the following example, the applicant is interested in moving up within the company.

> In last week's ***Bulletin***, I noticed that the position of administrative assistant for your department is now open. Could we schedule an interview to discuss the position? We could meet at your convenience, but my supervisor would prefer a Tuesday or Friday afternoon.
>
> For the past five years, I have worked for Mr. Gains in Catalog Sales. I began as a clerk-typist and have advanced to the position of secretary I. I have also completed several management courses at Twin Cities Community College.
>
> I look forward to talking with you to learn more about the position. A more complete review of my experience and education is on the attached résumé.

21:06 Keep these letters short. Readers often set long messages aside.

21:07 Ask a friend to read your letter. Another person can tell you whether your words flow naturally and make sense from the reader's point of view.

21:08 Be especially careful to avoid cover letter clichés. Phrases like "I am a dynamic self-starter with two feet on the ground and one eye on the horizon" tell the reader that you copied your letter from some poorly written find-a-job book.

2. INTERVIEW FOLLOW-UP NOTES

21:09 After a job interview, common courtesy and common sense require you to write a thank-you note to the interviewer. Mail it within 24 hours of the interview. Employers often hire the people who write interview follow-up notes (but write it even if you don't want the job).

21:10 This note can be as short as two or three sentences. Thank the interviewer and, to keep your note from looking like a thoughtless form letter, mention some important aspect of the interview. Here is an example.

> Thank you for meeting with me to discuss the opening in your hardware department. The position is exactly what I have in mind, and your commitment to customer support was especially impressive.
>
> I look forward to hearing from you soon.

21:11 Here is a note that the applicant wrote after deciding not to pursue the position.
> Please accept my thanks for a pleasant interview. I regret that obligations to my family prevent my taking a position requiring so much travel.
>
> Good luck to you and to AMZ Inc.

English for Professionals

3. RECOMMENDATIONS

21:12 Letters and memorandums of recommendation are among the most important messages you will write. They give you the opportunity to support a friend or to reward a deserving employee.

IMPORTANT NOTE: Always give a copy of the letter or memorandum to the person you are recommending. If something goes awry, you will not be suspected of foul play.

Follow these guidelines in recommending someone for a better job.

1. In the opening paragraph, establish your right to speak for the person you are recommending. Briefly state how long you have known the person, and describe your association. Also state that you are pleased to be writing the recommendation.

2. In the middle paragraphs, list the person's professional and personal qualities, and support those statements with specific examples. Details are important in recommendations. Be thorough but don't waste words.

3. Mention the person by name in every paragraph.

4. Close with a strong recommendation, and add a general statement encouraging the reader to hire that person.

21:13 Here is an example:

> For the past two years, I have known Joe Reed both professionally and personally. I have come to admire Joe as a manager and value him as a friend. I was pleased when he asked me to write you about his qualifications.
>
> Joe is one of the most conscientious people in our department. Last year's surprise audit found his books in excellent shape, and he won our unit's annual award for efficiency two years in a row.
>
> In addition, Joe is an excellent communicator. His subordinates understand and respect him, and his letters and reports are among the finest this office has ever produced.
>
> Joe Reed has my strongest recommendation. His skills and professionalism will make him an asset to anyone who employs him. You would, indeed, be fortunate to have Joe on your staff.

21:14 If an undeserving person asks you for a recommendation, you should decline. Gently suggest that the person approach someone else, someone who can write a more enthusiastic recommendation.

21:15 If you are obligated to write a recommendation for an undeserving person, follow the guidelines, but tone down your support. Dwell on the person's strong points, and ignore the weak points. Do not support your comments with examples, and make your closing recommendation lukewarm. Avoid sarcasm and negative comments.

21:16 The following letter recommends a less deserving Joe Reed.

> For the past two years, I have known Joe Reed both personally and professionally. I have learned to appreciate Joe's talents and character.
>
> Joe is a good man and a conscientious worker. His educational background is sound, and his experience includes such areas as accounting, data processing, and management.
>
> I recommend Joe for the position at AMZ Inc. He should be a productive member of your organization.

21:17 Another common recommendation is written when a supervisor recommends an employee for a raise or a promotion. Here are the guidelines.

1. Name the employee, and give the employee's current job title.

2. Say how long the employee has been with the company, and briefly trace the employee's history with the company.

3. State that the person deserves the raise or the promotion.

4. Give your justification for the raise or the promotion. Be thorough and include supporting details.

5. Name the position you want the employee to have, and if it's appropriate, give the recommended salary.

6. Close with strong support for the raise or the promotion.

21:18 The following memorandum uses these guidelines.

> Carol Webster, one of our word processing operators, has been with AMZ Inc for almost six years. She joined the company as a clerk-typist and was soon promoted to secretary II. Within two years, she became a word processing operator. She has held that position for eighteen months. I believe Carol has earned another promotion.
>
> Carol is the top operator in the department. Her keyboard speed is a consistent eighty-five words per minute, and her error rate is half the department average. She has excellent filing and shorthand skills and always maintains a helpful and patient attitude in dealing with her clients and fellow employees.
>
> Carol is one of the finest professionals at AMZ Inc. Her personality and skills qualify her for the position of secretary I. I strongly recommend that she be promoted and that the promotion take effect at the end of this month.

4. RESIGNATIONS

Most resignations are written under pleasant circumstances, when a person leaves a good position for a better one. At other times, they are written because a person is escaping an unbearable job or has been asked to resign. These two situations, pleasant and unpleasant, call for two distinct approaches to resignations.

PLEASANT RESIGNATIONS

A resignation written under pleasant circumstances resembles a thank-you note and follows these guidelines.

1. Use the indirect approach (explain first).

2. Stress the positive side of the situation, even if negative aspects exist. In being positive, avoid lies and sarcasm. You might have complaints or suggestions, but this letter or memorandum is probably not the place for them. Save those comments for an exit interview or a letter to a higher level of management.

3. State that you are resigning, and give the effective date. Express this information in pleasant terms in a long sentence that is part of a long paragraph.

4. Close by looking forward to continued good relations.

Here is an example of a resignation under pleasant circumstances.

> Work in the Advertising Department has been interesting and educational, and I have enjoyed being associated with so many good people.
>
> Last week, I was offered a position with another company. The offer is especially tempting since it involves working with advanced computer-aided drafting equipment. After careful consideration, I have decided to take the position and to submit my resignation effective June 14, 2005. As much as I regret leaving AMZ Inc, I am excited about my new responsibilities and the opportunities for professional growth.
>
> Thank you for two years of support and cooperation. If I can ever be of service to you, please call on me.

UNPLEASANT RESIGNATIONS

Resignations due to unpleasant circumstances follow these guidelines.

1. Do not explain, threaten, accuse, make excuses, or complain unless the situation demands it.

2. Politely state that you are resigning, and give the effective date.

5. DISMISSALS

21:22 Letters and memorandums of dismissal can be devastating. Good management principles dictate that they be written only after reasonable efforts have been made to counsel an employee or to move the employee into a more suitable position. When the situation is handled properly, the dismissal will surprise no one.

21:23 When an employee is dismissed due to incompetence, the message can be a simple notification of the dismissal and its effective date. Depending on your company's policy or your personal preference, you might or might not give a reason for the dismissal.

21:24 IMPORTANT NOTE: Before you write a message dismissing someone for incompetence, discuss your message with a lawyer or with an upper-level manager in your company. A botched dismissal can lead to a lawsuit.

21:25 Not all dismissals are a result of an employee's incompetence. A position could be the victim of automation or other economic trends. When a valued employee must be dismissed, the dismissal notice should explain the situation. Perhaps the reader understands the circumstances and expects to be laid off, but this letter or memorandum documents the unfortunate situation. It might comfort the employee and help in the search for a new job.

21:26 In such cases, use the indirect approach (explain first). Leave no doubt that the employee is being dismissed, and give the effective date of the dismissal. Here is an example.

> Our corporation is in a time of crisis. Deficit spending, a strong dollar, and trade imbalances have nearly destroyed industries like ours.
>
> During the last two years, new orders have declined by 39 percent, and our profits have turned to losses. As a result, we are forced to make reductions in personnel. We have studied the situation carefully, but no alternative exists. The position you hold will be deleted effective October 1, 2006. We wish we could move you into another position, but we have no openings. We will, however, provide you with recommendations as you seek other employment.
>
> You have been an asset to our company, and you have every right to be proud of your record with AMZ Inc. We regret losing such a valuable employee, but we are confident that a person with your skills and character will easily find employment with a more promising future.

6. CONGRATULATORY NOTES

21:27   Follow these guidelines in writing letters, memorandums, and e-mails of congratulations.

   1. Send the note within a few days of the event. If the note is late because the news was slow in reaching you, mention that fact to the reader.

   2. Use a relaxed, informal tone, but make sure the note is written on a word processor and is in a proper business format.

   3. Consider mentioning one of the person's outstanding traits, but avoid flattery.

   4. Keep it short.

   5. Don't send the message unless you have worked with the person or have established a friendly relationship. Congratulatory notes don't ordinarily come from strangers.

21:28   Here is an example.

   Your promotion to assistant personnel manager was welcome news. I have long admired your ability to work with people and am always delighted to see a good guy move up.

   All of us in Sales look forward to working with you.

7. THANK-YOU LETTERS, MEMORANDUMS, AND E-MAILS

21:29   For personal thank-you notes, refer to a book on personal etiquette. For business thank-you notes, use standard business stationery and standard letter, memorandum, or e-mail format, and follow these guidelines.

   1. Open with a general comment of appreciation that strongly hints at *thank you*, but don't use the words *thank you*.

   2. Mention one or more specific points about the event that caused you to write this note.

   3. Conclude with another general statement that clearly says *thank you*.

21:30   Here is an example.

   Elizabeth and I had a wonderful stay in Montreal, and the evening we spent with you and Jean Paul was the high point of our trip.

   Our guided tour of your beautiful city, dinner at La Maison de Michelle, and the evening at the symphony combined to create an evening we will never forget.

   Thank you for turning a routine business trip into a dream come true.

WORDS OF CAUTION

21:31   The guidelines in this chapter provide you, the writer, with a place to start, but they cannot deal adequately with all possible situations. Use these guidelines, but never hesitate to modify them to meet your specific requirements.

21:32 **TOPICS FOR DISCUSSION**

1. Did you write an interview follow-up note after your most recent job interview? What effect should such a note have on a prospective employer?

2. Why must a supervisor know how to write convincing recommendations?

3. What might happen if you tell the whole truth in a letter of recommendation you write for an undeserving person?

4. Have you ever resigned from a position? Did you submit a letter of resignation? If so, would the guidelines in this chapter have improved it?

5. Have you ever been involved in the dismissal of an incompetent employee? If so, was the situation handled as well as it might have been?

21:33 **EXERCISE 21**
SPECIAL LETTERS

1. Think of a special letter not discussed in this chapter. Set up your own guidelines for writing it.

2. Find special letters you have written or received. Would the guidelines in this chapter have improved them?

3. Write a letter of application (résumé cover letter) for a job or a promotion you would like to have.

4. Write a letter recommending your best friend for a suitable position.

22 PROOFREADING SKILLS

22:01   Everyone makes mistakes. People who can produce a single perfect document are rare, but your writing must be as nearly perfect as you can make it. To write well, you must develop proofreading skills.

Unfortunately, proofreading is not easy, especially when you proofread your own work.

When you write, you write in two places, on the paper or screen and in your mind. As you write, your mind forms a mental image of the document. In your mind's eye, the writing is perfect.

On the paper, however, your hand struggles to keep pace with your speeding brain. It omits words, reverses letters, and makes other careless errors. (Why do we call such mistakes *careless errors* when we *care* greatly and would give almost anything to stop making them?)

When you finish writing and check for errors, they are hard to find. Your eyes are on your paper, but your mind prefers to read its own mental image of the document. To force your mind to concentrate on the paper, you must escape the mental image. Each trick of the proofreader's trade is based on some method of blotting out that mental image.

USING COMPUTERS

22:02   If you use a computer to do your writing, it can help you proofread. Most word processors have spelling checkers. Grammar checkers might also help if you know enough about grammar and usage to ignore most of their suggestions.

Another way to proofread with a computer is to use the "search" function. If, for example, you have trouble with the words *affect* and *effect* (13:03), complete your document, and then search for those words to check the usage. If you have a tendency to abuse passive voice (17:06), search for *by*. Keep a "prooflist" of your habitual errors. It will help you find your errors, and it might eventually teach you to avoid them.

Learning to use a word processor takes time, but the time saved in proofreading and revising will make it worth your effort. Letting your computer check for mistakes should be the first step in your proofreading routine.

DEPENDING ON YOURSELF

22:03   Next, do the best you can to find errors on your own. Try to push your mental image of the document aside so you can see what is on the page. These three strategies will help.

22:04   1. Reading with a Straightedge
One way to shatter the mental image is to use a straightedge (a ruler, a piece of cardboard or plastic, or a blank sheet of typing paper that is simply folded in half).

When you want to proofread something, set the document on your desk. Place the straightedge just under the first line you want to check. Read it carefully. Then move on to the next line. As you move down the page, you will see each line in isolation, and the straightedge will keep your eyes from speeding carelessly ahead. Force yourself to read slowly.

22:05   **2. Goofy Reading**
Another good way to find your own errors involves reading your document aloud while making your voice sound ridiculous.

Pretend to be a computer, and read each syllable with the same dull tone. The information will be clear enough, but goofy reading will force you to look more carefully at each word.

If you have a straightedge handy, use it too. Goofy reading while using a straightedge is probably the most effective way to proofread something you have just written.

22:06   **3. Letting Time Pass**
Finally, lay your document aside, and check it later.

As time passes, your mental image will fade. Five minutes is better than nothing, but try to allow hours or even days to pass.

When you write something especially important, a letter of application for example, write it several days early, and put it out of sight. Don't look at it until the time comes to proofread it. Then correct it and send it out.

22:07   Every time you proofread, convince yourself that the mistakes are there. The challenge lies in finding them. Never be surprised when you find a mistake. Be surprised when you don't.

22:08   Always proofread your document three times:
- Read it once to check your spelling and punctuation.
- Read it again to concentrate on clarity and style.
- Read it a final time to look for words that can be culled (18:27).

INVOLVING OTHER PEOPLE

22:09   The best way to avoid the mental image of your document is to let other people proofread for you.

Other people have no choice but to look at the words on the paper, and they sometimes find errors resulting from your lack of knowledge. Other people can also help you spot sentences that might not be clear to your reader.

Pick good writers. Good writers understand the importance of proofreading.

Consider forming a proofreading alliance with a respected colleague. You can take turns checking each other's work, and you will enjoy learning from each other and settling friendly disputes.

Never be embarrassed to ask others to proofread your work. Professional writers do it all the time.

WORDS OF CAUTION

22:10   Too much emphasis on proofreading can seriously reduce productivity. A recent study at a major university found that, contrary to expectations, some newly installed word processors actually reduced productivity. The word processors, the researchers discovered, made proofreading and revising almost fun, and some people were spending hours on a single letter.

Important documents, like résumés and recommendations, must be proofread with the greatest care, but routine correspondence should never be revised and reprinted more than once. Proofread the document once on the screen. Then print it, and give it three more quick readings (use your straightedge and goofy reading). Make your changes, print it a second time, and send it out. If you know how to proofread, you can do the job quickly.

23 IMPROVING YOUR ENGLISH

23:01　As surely as we are human, we are condemned to imperfection. As we speak and write, we are too frequently reminded of that fact. Still, you *can* improve your English. You have the ability to speak and to write far better than the average professional if only you will keep trying.

CORRECTING BAD HABITS

23:02　Here are four easy steps you can follow to stop making a specific error in your spoken or written English.

STEP 1
Discover that you make the error.

> This first step is more difficult than you might imagine. Few people are aware of their own faults. Remain vigilant, and hope others will care enough to help you spot your errors.
>
> Taking the pretest at the end of this book is an excellent way to identify your errors.

STEP 2
Post a note with the error on it.

> Somewhere around your work area, put up a card identifying the error. Place it where you will notice it frequently.

STEP 3
Look for opportunities to avoid that specific error.

> Use the proper form at least three times a day for seven days, and give yourself credit on the card you posted. If opportunities don't appear on their own, create them.

STEP 4
After the seven days of practice have passed (STEP 3), watch yourself carefully for two weeks.

> If you backslide, go back to STEP 3. If you have stopped making the error, take down your card, date it, and file it away for future reference. Now go on to another error.

REPROGRAMMING YOUR BEHAVIOR

23:03　Most of our linguistic patterns were established when we were children. Some psychologists believe we can alter those patterns by frequently reminding ourselves that we want to change. Find a time in your daily routine when you can stand in front of a mirror and repeat this phrase.

Speak clearly and speak standard English.

Look yourself in the eye, be polite, and speak quietly. Repeat the phrase as many as ten times. The process could take weeks, months, or even years, but standard English will eventually become your normal mode of expression.

DEVELOPING THE RIGHT ATTITUDE

23:04 Improving your English will be a lifelong task. If you handle yourself well, it can be fun. If you become vain and pompous, you will make yourself and the people around you miserable. The critical factor is your attitude. These ten guidelines will help.

1. **Care.**
   If you are reading this book, you probably care. Take pride in your English just as you take pride in your work, your home, and your appearance.

2. **Don't trust your ears.**
   Never be surprised when something that sounds correct is wrong. It simply means you have been making that mistake for a long time.

3. **Make friends with a dictionary.**
   Read the introductory articles, look over the appendixes, and learn to use the pronunciation symbols.

4. **Make friends with a good handbook.**
   No one knows everything about English usage. Experts are people who know how to look things up.

5. **Prufread carefuly.**
   Often, proofreading makes the difference between a good writer and a poor writer.

6. **Take pleasure in discovering your mistakes.**
   Everyone makes mistakes, but you can be proud that you do something about yours.

7. **Take pleasure in discovering the mistakes of others, but don't look down on those who make them.**
   Good English is the product of training, not intelligence. Never scold. Offer to help if you can do so gracefully.

8. **Read good writing.**
   As you read well-written English, that computer inside your head will magically absorb the rules of grammar and the principles of good sentence structure.

9. **Feel free to speak your dialect around your family and childhood friends.**
   Dialects are nothing to be ashamed of. They simply aren't appropriate at work.

10. **NEVER underestimate the intelligence of a person who speaks a dialect.**
    Dialects are as difficult to learn as standard English, and the person speaking a dialect could easily be smarter than you are.

23:05 ## TOPICS FOR DISCUSSION

1. Which of your English errors will you work on first?

2. Has your English ever embarrassed you? Explain.

3. Have you known well-trained, talented professionals whose careers suffered because of their English?

4. Have you known people who succeeded in spite of poor English skills?

5. What are English dialects? Where did they come from?

24 REFERENCE BOOKS

24:01 As a business writer, you might want these reference books on or near your desk. They are listed in order of declining importance. The prices given here were current when this book went to press.

24:02 1. *Merriam-Webster's Collegiate Dictionary*, eleventh edition
(ISBN 0-87779-809-5), $24. (Expect it to be sold for as little as $15.)
or
24:03 *The American Heritage College Dictionary*, fourth edition
(ISBN 0-618-83595-4), $29. (Expect it to be discounted to about $20.)

Traditionally, **Merriam-Webster** has been the American standard. **American Heritage** is, however, more carefully edited, and it offers more advice in the area of proper usage.

Many other good dictionaries are on the market. If you have a good one, keep it. If your dictionary is more than ten years old, replace it.

24:04 2. *The Gregg Reference Manual*, tenth edition, by William A. Sabin
(ISBN 0-07-313348-5), $47 for the spiral-bound version. (Many dealers charge $35.)

Gregg is the recognized authority in business writing. This handbook covers proper usage thoroughly and shows how to format letters, memorandums, e-mails, and reports. No one who writes for business, industry, or government should be without one. It is definitely worth the price.

Buy the spiral-bound version. It's less expensive than the hardback or paperback versions and will lie open on your desk.

24:05 3. *The Chicago Manual of Style*, fifteenth edition
(ISBN 0-226-10403-6), $55. (Expect to find it for about $35.)

This authoritative book is written for the publishing industry, not for business writers. Still, it provides a wealth of information that applies to both.

24:06 4. *A Dictionary of Modern English Usage*, by H. W. Fowler
(ISBN 0-19-860506-4), $16.

Fowler is a classic. It touches on the finer points of usage. If **Merriam-Webster**, **American Heritage**, and **Gregg** can't help, try **Fowler**.

24:07 5. *Understanding English Grammar*, eighth edition, by Martha Kolln
(ISBN 0-20562690-4), $107.

People who are interested in traditional grammar and who don't already own a good book on the subject might try this one. It's thorough and understandable, and it uses sentence diagramming.

24:08 If you still use your English handbook from high school or college, put it away. It was written to help students write academic papers. Its focus is probably too narrow for business professionals.

24:08   If you still use your English handbook from high school or college, put it away. It was written to help students write academic papers. Its focus is probably too narrow for business professionals.

24:09   **TOPICS FOR DISCUSSION**

1. Where do dictionaries come from? Who decides what passes for standard English and what doesn't?

2. Are you familiar with the *Oxford English Dictionary*? What type of dictionary is it?

3. Do you have a favorite English handbook? If so, describe it.

APPENDIX A: PRETEST

This test will help you learn more about your business writing skills and will show you which chapters in *CommonSense Grammar and Style* you need to study. (Several chapters are not represented on the pretest because they teach concepts that can't be tested using this format.)

Each item in the test asks you to choose between two statements, *a* and *b*.

Sometimes you are asked to choose one sentence that represents better grammar or better style than another. These sentences are presented in normal print. Here is an example. (The critical differences are underlined to help you work more quickly.)

   a.   We appreciate your taking the time to help.
   b.   We appreciate you taking the time to help.
   c.   I don't know which one is better.

At other times, you are asked to choose a statement more nearly true than another. These statements are set in bold type. Look at this example:

   a.   **A letter with plenty of white space is easier to read.**
   b.   **A letter with minimal white space is easier to read.**
   c.   I don't know which one is more nearly true.

If you can choose *a* or *b* with confidence, write *a* or *b* on the answer sheet, and go on to the next item. If you are not reasonably certain which one is better, write *c* on the answer sheet.

Don't try to improve your performance by guessing. Guessing could prevent you from seeking help when you need it. When in doubt, choose *c*.

Even when you are fairly certain of an answer, you might circle c simply because you want to read more about the topic.

Don't be discouraged if several items *appear* to test the same concept. They don't.

When you have completed the pretest, check your answers. The answers, arranged according to chapter, are on the pages following the pretest. Incorrect choices and *c*'s point to the chapters you should study first.

SUGGESTION: Photocopy the *answer sheet* following this page, and use it to record your selections. It allows you to check your work quickly.

> **WARNING: You will need several hours to complete this pretest. Do not try to take this entire test in one sitting.**

ANSWER SHEET

(Photocopy this page, and fill in your answers as you take the pretest.)

CAUTION: When you check your answers, don't mark your mistakes and c's on this page. Instead, mark them on the pages called "Answers to the Pretest."

1. ___	30. ___	59. ___	88. ___	117. ___	147. ___	177. ___
2. ___	31. ___	60. ___	89. ___	118. ___	148. ___	178. ___
3. ___	32. ___	61. ___	90. ___	119. ___	149. ___	179. ___
4. ___	33. ___	62. ___	91. ___	120. ___	150. ___	180. ___
5. ___	34. ___	63. ___	92. ___	121. ___	151. ___	181. ___
6. ___	35. ___	64. ___	93. ___	122. ___	152. ___	182. ___
7. ___	36. ___	65. ___	94. ___	123. ___	153. ___	183. ___
8. ___	37. ___	66. ___	95. ___	124. ___	154. ___	184. ___
9. ___	38. ___	67. ___	96. ___	125. ___	155. ___	185. ___
10. ___	39. ___	68. ___	97. ___	126. ___	156. ___	186. ___
11. ___	40. ___	69. ___	98. ___	127. ___	157. ___	187. ___
12. ___	41. ___	70. ___	99. ___	128. ___	158. ___	188. ___
13. ___	42. ___	71. ___	100. ___	129. ___	159. ___	189. ___
14. ___	43. ___	72. ___	101. ___	130. ___	160. ___	190. ___
15. ___	44. ___	73. ___	102. ___	131. ___	161. ___	191. ___
16. ___	45. ___	74. ___	103. ___	132. ___	162. ___	192. ___
17. ___	46. ___	75. ___	104. ___	133. ___	163. ___	193. ___
18. ___	47. ___	76. ___	105. ___	134. ___	164. ___	194. ___
19. ___	48. ___	77. ___	106. ___	135. ___	165. ___	195. ___
20. ___	49. ___	78. ___	107. ___	136. ___	166. ___	196. ___
21. ___	50. ___	79. ___	108. ___	137. ___	167. ___	197. ___
22. ___	51. ___	80. ___	109. ___	138. ___	168. ___	198. ___
23. ___	52. ___	81. ___	110. ___	139. ___	169. ___	199. ___
24. ___	53. ___	82. ___	111. ___	140. ___	170. ___	200. ___
25. ___	54. ___	83. ___	112. ___	141. ___	171. ___	201. ___
26. ___	55. ___	84. ___	113. ___	142. ___	172. ___	202. ___
27. ___	56. ___	85. ___	114. ___	143. ___	173. ___	203. ___
28. ___	57. ___	86. ___	115. ___	144. ___	174. ___	204. ___
29. ___	58. ___	87. ___	116. ___	145. ___	175. ___	205. ___
				146. ___	176. ___	206. ___

English for Professionals 127

Remember, the critical differences are underlined to help you work more quickly. (Commas and semicolons have the underlining on either side to leave them clearly visible.)

1. a. We ordered 2 hamburgers and 3 milk shakes. (7:02)
   b. We ordered two hamburgers and three milk shakes.
   c. I don't know which one is better.

2. a. Three people were there: Ted Saltz, Steve Pershaw, and Holly Carmack. (5:02)
   b. Three people were there, Ted Saltz, Steve Pershaw, and Holly Carmack.
   c. I don't know which one is better.

3. a. Her six-year-old daughter is in the first grade. (15:09)
   b. Her six year old daughter is in the first grade.
   c. I don't know which one is better.

4. a. **Business writers should not use pronouns like I, me, and my.** (18:02)
   b. **Business writers should use pronouns like I, me, and my.**
   c. I don't know which one is more nearly true.

5. a. About six hundred people helped pay for the new beds. (7:02)
   b. About 600 people helped pay for the new beds.
   c. I don't know which one is better.

6. a. Mickey lacks formal training in design yet he seldom makes a mistake. (3:02)
   b. Mickey lacks formal training in design, yet he seldom makes a mistake.
   c. I don't know which one is better.

7. a. We have organized an international conference. (13:02)
   b. We have organized a international conference.
   c. I don't know which one is better.

8. a. Tell the Sheriff that the Mayor will be in tomorrow. (6:03)
   b. Tell the sheriff that the mayor will be in tomorrow.
   c. I don't know which one is better.

9. a. They have done alot of work this evening. (14:03)
   b. They have done a lot of work this evening.
   c. I don't know which one is better.

10. a. Me and Wilbur left early for lunch. (2:02)
    b. Wilbur and I left early for lunch.
    c. I don't know which one is better.

11. a. Please take the memo to Mary and ask her to respond this afternoon. (3:02)
    b. Please take the memo to Mary, and ask her to respond this afternoon.
    c. I don't know which one is better.

12. a. **Business writers should not use words like you and yours to refer to specific people.** (18:03)
    b. **Business writers should use words like you and yours to refer to specific people.**
    c. I don't know which one is more nearly true.

13. a. We live in an universe that continues to mystify us. (13:02)
    b. We live in a universe that continues to mystify us.
    c. I don't know which one is better.

14. a. A small group of tourists is waiting for the bus. (1:02)
    b. A small group of tourists are waiting for the bus.
    c. I don't know which one is better.

15. a. **We can <u>emphasize</u> an important point by stating that it's important.** (19:02)
    b. **Stating that something is important actually <u>de-emphasizes</u> it.**
    c. I don't know which one is more nearly true.

16. a. Will the Smother<u>s</u> (Mr. and Ms. Smothers) be in town this weekend? (11:04)
    b. Will the Smother<u>ses</u> (Mr. an Ms. Smothers) be in town this weekend?
    c. I don't know which one is better.

17. a. **In business writing, <u>short, simple sentences</u> are usually better than long ones.** (18:04)
    b. **In business writing, <u>long, complex sentences</u> are usually better than short ones.**
    c. I don't know which one is more nearly true.

18. a. She gave the awards to<u>:</u> Chuck Hays, Patsy Drew, and Nadia Markovich. (5:03)
    b. She gave the awards to Chuck Hays, Patsy Drew, and Nadia Markovich.
    c. I don't know which one is better.

19. a. At that point, the trail ends with a <u>15-or-16-foot</u> drop to the river. (15:08)
    b. At that point, the trail ends with a <u>15- or 16-foot</u> drop to the river.
    c. I don't know which one is better.

20. a. The boo<u>ks</u> cover is torn. (12:03)
    b. The boo<u>k's</u> cover is torn.
    c. I don't know which one is better.

21. a. The lightning is <u>affecting</u> our ability to navigate. (13:03)
    b. The lightning is <u>effecting</u> our ability to navigate.
    c. I don't know which one is better.

22. a. Our new supervisor, Edgar Goss, came b<u>y,</u> and he asked Cheri, Edward, and James to meet with him tomorrow afternoon. (4:03)
    b. Our new supervisor, Edgar Goss, came b<u>y;</u> and he asked Cheri, Edward, and James to meet with him tomorrow afternoon.
    c. I don't know which one is better.

23. a. If Lucy wants to drive, it's <u>all right</u> with me. (14:04)
    b. If Lucy wants to drive, it's <u>alright</u> with me.
    c. I don't know which one is better.

24. a. **In business writing, <u>five-sentence paragraphs are probably too long</u>.** (18:05)
    b. **In business writing, <u>all paragraphs should be at least three sentences long</u>.**
    c. I don't know which one is more nearly true.

25. a. **Business writing normally uses <u>active voice</u>.** (17:04 and 18:19)
    b. **Business writing normally uses <u>passive voice</u>.**
    c. I don't know which one is more nearly true.

26. a. The satellite surveyed <u>12 million</u> acres in one week. (7:05)
    b. The satellite surveyed <u>12,000,000</u> acres in one week.
    c. I don't know which one is better.

27. a. The <u>number</u> of well-written letters she produces is amazing. (13:05)
    b. The <u>amount</u> of well-written letters she produces is amazing.
    c. I don't know which one is better.

English for Professionals 129

28. a. We tested six new software packages but did not find one we could use. (3:04)
    b. We tested six new software packages, but did not find one we could use.
    c. I don't know which one is better.

29. a. In the winter, <u>fewer</u> people visit the park. (13:06)
    b. In the winter, <u>less</u> people visit the park.
    c. I don't know which one is better.

30. a. <u>Whom</u> is she waiting for? (8:02)
    b. <u>Who</u> is she waiting for?
    c. I don't know which one is better.

31. a. <u>Everyone</u> of our representatives is ready to go to work. (13:07)
    b. <u>Every one</u> of our representatives is ready to go to work.
    c. I don't know which one is better.

32. a. We presented our proposal to <u>C</u>ouncilman Rodriguez. (6:02)
    b. We presented our proposal to <u>c</u>ouncilman Rodriguez.
    c. I don't know which one is better.

33. a. **Business writers <u>should use</u> one-sentence paragraphs without hesitation.** (18:06)
    b. **Business writers <u>should avoid</u> one-sentence paragraphs.**
    c. I don't know which one is more nearly true.

34. a. The hospital needs <u>3</u> more physicians and <u>14</u> more registered nurses. (7:03)
    b. The hospital needs <u>three</u> more physicians and <u>fourteen</u> more registered nurses.
    c. I don't know which one is better.

35. a. Did you put our meeting on your <u>calender</u>? (14:05)
    b. Did you put our meeting on your <u>calendar</u>?
    c. I don't know which one is better.

36. a. Dr Long and <u>I</u> will attend the conference. (2:02)
    b. Dr Long and <u>me</u> will attend the conference.
    c. I don't know which one is better.

37. a. A <u>well-dressed</u> man sat by the window. (15:10)
    b. A <u>well dressed</u> man sat by the window.
    c. I don't know which one is better.

38. a. The Higgins<u>'</u> new house is beautiful. (12:10)
    b. The Higgins<u>'s</u> new house is beautiful.
    c. I don't know which one is better.

39. a. He worked two jobs so that he could put his daughter through college. (3:06)
    b. He worked two jobs, so that he could put his daughter through college.
    c. I don't know which one is better.

40. a. I can <u>assure</u> you that the parts will be delivered on time. (13:08)
    b. I can <u>ensure</u> you that the parts will be delivered on time.
    c. I don't know which one is better.

41. a. These days, one of those machines <u>cost</u> over $40,000. (11:06)
    b. These days, one of those machines <u>costs</u> over $40,000.
    c. I don't know which one is better.

42. a. **Use professional jargon (terms unique to your profession) anytime a situation calls for it. It's a good way to impress people.** (18:08)
    b. **Avoid professional jargon unless you are working with other members of your profession. It can confuse people outside your profession.**
    c. I don't know which one is more nearly true.

43. a. Claire is taller than he is. (10:02)
    b. Claire is more tall than he is.
    c. I don't know which one is better.

44. a. None of the passengers was hurt. (1:03)
    b. None of the passengers were hurt.
    c. I don't know which one is better.

45. a. They have done everything possible to assure success. (13:08)
    b. They have done everything possible to ensure success.
    c. I don't know which one is better.

46. a. Each of his victories was hard-won. (15:22)
    b. Each of his victories was hard won.
    c. I don't know which one is better.

47. a. How many videoes did she take to the trade show? (11:07)
    b. How many videos did she take to the trade show?
    c. I don't know which one is better.

48. a. She transferred to Los Angeles so she could be near her parents. (3:06)
    b. She transferred to Los Angeles, so she could be near her parents.
    c. I don't know which one is better.

49. a. **We should avoid legal terms in routine business correspondence.** (18:09)
    b. **Legal terminology is part of the business world** and should be used in business correspondence.
    c. I don't know which one is more nearly true.

50. a. Every American President has had problems with Congress. (6:04)
    b. Every American president has had problems with Congress.
    c. I don't know which one is better.

51. a. They live on Harding Road in Lubbock, TX. (9:03)
    b. They live on Harding Road in Lubbock, Texas.
    c. I don't know which one is better.

52. a. My brothers and I divided the winnings between ourselves. (13:10)
    b. My brothers and I divided the winnings among ourselves.
    c. I don't know which one is better.

53. a. They sent copies of the plans to Nancy and I. (2:02)
    b. They sent copies of the plans to Nancy and me.
    c. I don't know which one is better.

54. a. The elderly couple helped one another up the stairs. (13:11)
    b. The elderly couple helped each other up the stairs.
    c. I don't know which one is better.

English for Professionals 131

55. a. She <u>can not</u> go with us if we leave this morning. (14:06)
    b. She <u>cannot</u> go with us if we leave this morning.
    c. I don't know which one is better.

56. a. <u>Twenty</u> people volunteered to shovel sand. (7:06)
    b. <u>20</u> people volunteered to shovel sand.
    c. I don't know which one is better.

57. a. <u>May</u> I borrow your tent for the camping trip? (13:12)
    b. <u>Can</u> I borrow your tent for the camping trip?
    c. I don't know which one is better.

58. a. Before we flew back from Alask<u>a,</u> we went fishing along the coast. (3:07)
    b. Before we flew back from Alaska we went fishing along the coast.
    c. I don't know which one is better.

59. **a. Repeating an important point at the end of a letter <u>could offend your reader</u>.** (19:03)
    b. Repeating an important point at the end of a letter <u>emphasizes the point</u>.
    c. I don't know which one is more nearly true.

60. a. As the interview proceeded, she felt more <u>self-confident</u>. (15:11)
    b. As the interview proceeded, she felt more <u>selfconfident</u>.
    c. I don't know which one is better.

61. a. <u>Who</u> prepared the presentation for last week's board meeting? (8:04)
    b. <u>Whom</u> prepared the presentation for last week's board meeting?
    c. I don't know which one is better.

62. a. Joan <u>and/or</u> her father will be here soon. (18:10)
    b. Joan <u>or</u> her father will be here soon.
    c. I don't know which one is better.

63. a. They seem to have arrived at <u>a consensus of opinion</u>. (13:13)
    b. They seem to have arrived at <u>a consensus</u>.
    c. I don't know which one is better.

64. a. The desk is made of the following woods: (5:05)
       Walnut<u>.</u>
       Cherry<u>.</u>
       Poplar<u>.</u>

    b. The desk is made of the following woods:
       walnut<u>,</u>
       cherry<u>,</u>
       poplar<u>.</u>

    c. I don't know which one is better.

65. a. <u>Who</u> will your aunt be visiting? (8:04)
    b. <u>Whom</u> will your aunt be visiting?
    c. I don't know which one is better.

66. a. We've <u>done</u> agreed to take her. (13:16)
    b. We've <u>already</u> agreed to take her.
    c. I don't know which one is better.

67. a. The President of our firm has a sister, and she is my Department Head. (6:05)
    b. The president of our firm has a sister, and she is my department head.
    c. I don't know which one is better.

68. a. The truck which we drove to Denver needs new tires. (13:27 and 18:11)
    b. The truck that we drove to Denver needs new tires.
    c. I don't know which one is better.

69. a. Several thousand delegates attended the conference. (7:08)
    b. Several 1,000s of delegates attended the conference.
    c. I don't know which one is better.

70. a. His birthday is in February. (14:07)
    b. His birthday is in Febuary.
    c. I don't know which one is better.

71. a. Frank ordered new keyboards for me and Evelyn. (2:03)
    b. Frank ordered new keyboards for Evelyn and me.
    c. I don't know which one is better.

72. a. **Placing information at the beginning or end of a letter emphasizes the information.** (19:04)
    b. **Placing information at the beginning or end of a letter de-emphasizes the information.**
    c. I don't know which one is more nearly true.

73. a. They have hired a team of five attornies. (11:10)
    b. They have hired a team of five attorneys.
    c. I don't know which one is better.

74. a. Her writing style is quite different from Henry's. (13:14)
    b. Her writing style is quite different than Henry's.
    c. I don't know which one is better.

75. a. We invited them to the barbecue our company organized, because they will be working with several of our engineers. (3:09)
    b. We invited them to the barbecue our company organized because they will be working with several of our engineers.
    c. I don't know which one is better.

76. a. Mitch Fuller, the man who you talked to on the phone, is the manager. (8:05)
    b. Mitch Fuller, the man whom you talked to on the phone, is the manager.
    c. I don't know which one is better.

77. a. Do you keep a list of the companies we do business with? (18:12)
    b. Do you keep a list of the companies with which we do business?
    c. I don't know which one is better.

78. a. We worked on the problem everyday last week. (13:17)
    b. We worked on the problem every day last week.
    c. I don't know which one is better.

79. a. Our hastily-arranged meeting went well. (15:13)
    b. Our hastily arranged meeting went well.
    c. I don't know which one is better.

English for Professionals 133

80. a. Kaye earned her degree from Yale; Wesley's is from Arkansas State. (4:07)
    b. Kaye earned her degree from Yale, Wesley's is from Arkansas State.
    c. I don't know which one is better.

81. a. If I <u>were</u> in London, I would visit St Paul's Cathedral. (16:07)
    b. If I <u>was</u> in London, I would visit St Paul's Cathedral.
    c. I don't know which one is better.

82. a. Before you leave for Tucson, please review the following documents: (5:05)
       The instructions for running the end-of-the-year report
       Last year's end-of-the-year report
       The proposed changes to next year's report

    b. Before you leave for Tucson, please review the following documents:
       The instructions for running the end-of-the-year report,
       Last year's end-of-the-year report,
       The proposed changes to next year's report.

    c. I don't know which one is better.

83. a. The news media <u>has</u> questioned the truth of that statement. (1:04)
    b. The news media <u>have</u> questioned the truth of that statement.
    c. I don't know which one is better.

84. a. At least <u>8 percent</u> of our employees are sick today. (7:07)
    b. At least <u>eight percent</u> of our employees are sick today.
    c. I don't know which one is better.

85. a. The <u>squadron leaders'</u> reception was rescheduled. (15:14)
    b. The <u>squadron-leaders'</u> reception was rescheduled.
    c. I don't know which one is better.

86. a. Let's drive a little <u>further</u> down the road. (13:18)
    b. Let's drive a little <u>farther</u> down the road.
    c. I don't know which one is better.

87. a. I <u>will</u> be happy to review your prospectus. (18:13)
    b. I <u>shall</u> be happy to review your prospectus.
    c. I don't know which one is better.

88. a. Drop in on May, and if she can still see well enough to read, give her this book. (3:10)
    b. Drop in on May, and if she can still see well enough to read give her this book.
    c. I don't know which one is better.

89. a. Let's wait until <u>your</u> feeling better. (14:08)
    b. Let's wait until <u>you're</u> feeling better.
    c. I don't know which one is better.

90. a. Robin's comments could not have been <u>more rational</u>. (10:04)
    b. Robin's comments could not have been <u>rationaler</u>.
    c. I don't know which one is better.

91. a. Cindy is almost as tall as <u>I</u>. (2:04)
    b. Cindy is almost as tall as <u>me</u>.
    c. I don't know which one is better.

92. a. <u>Irregardless</u> of the storm, she went to work. (13:19)
　　b. <u>Regardless</u> of the storm, she went to work.
　　c. I don't know which one is better.

93. a. The <u>quality of the fleece</u> is exceptionally high this season. (12:12)
　　b. The <u>fleece's quality</u> is exceptionally high this season.
　　c. I don't know which one is better.

94. a. Did you ever find out <u>whom</u> the man in the car was? (8:06-07)
　　b. Did you ever find out <u>who</u> the man in the car was?
　　c. I don't know which one is better.

95. a. He asked her to <u>lend</u> him enough to make the down payment. (13:20)
　　b. He asked her to <u>loan</u> him enough to make the down payment.
　　c. I don't know which one is better.

96. a. She plays the piano, the oboe and the trumpet. (3:11-12)
　　b. She plays the piano, the oboe, and the trumpet.
　　c. I don't know which one is better.

97. a. <u>Most</u> of the meeting was spent discussing the new project. (13:21)
　　b. <u>The majority</u> of the meeting was spent discussing the new project.
　　c. I don't know which one is better.

98. a. Choose <u>whomever</u> you want to go with you. (8:08)
　　b. Choose <u>whoever</u> you want to go with you.
　　c. I don't know which one is better.

99. a. The <u>party</u> who ordered it lives in Georgia. (13:22)
　　b. The <u>person</u> who ordered it lives in Georgia.
　　c. I don't know which one is better.

100. a. By the end of the year: (5:06)
　　　　We must establish a positive cash flow.
　　　　The board must hire a permanent CEO.
　　　　The accountants must minimize our corporate taxes.
　　　　We must bring our computer systems up to date.

　　b. By the end of the year:
　　　　We must establish a positive cash flow
　　　　The board must hire a permanent CEO
　　　　The accountants must minimized our corporate taxes
　　　　We must bring our computer systems up to date

　　c. I don't know which one is better.

101. a. We spoke to several <u>people</u> about the purchase. (13:23)
　　 b. We spoke to several <u>persons</u> about the purchase.
　　 c. I don't know which one is better.

102. a. She sold her car because <u>it's</u> ten years old and <u>its</u> engine is worn-out. (14:09)
　　 b. She sold her car because <u>its</u> ten years old and <u>it's</u> engine is worn-out.
　　 c. I don't know which one is better.

103. a. The <u>principle</u> of the loan is around $10,000. (13:24)
　　 b. The <u>principal</u> of the loan is around $10,000.
　　 c. I don't know which one is better.

English for Professionals **135**

104. a. He can work faster than me. (2:04)
    b. He can work faster than I.
    c. I don't know which one is better.

105. a. Their long-term real estate investments record is impressive. (18:14)
    b. Their record for making long-term profits with real estate is impressive.
    c. I don't know which one is better.

106. a. About one-fourth of our employees completed the training. (7:09)
    b. About ¼ of our employees completed the training.
    c. I don't know which one is better.

107. a. A small, frightened child stood at her door. (3:13)
    b. A small frightened child stood at her door.
    c. I don't know which one is better.

108. a. Douglas has never been a man to stand on principle. (13:24)
    b. Douglas has never been a man to stand on principal.
    c. I don't know which one is better.

109. a. That satellite shines more brightly than Venus. (10:06)
    b. That satellite shines brighter than Venus.
    c. I don't know which one is better.

110. a. This is the problem with liability insurance. (18:15)
    b. This problem is associated with liability insurance.
    c. I don't know which one is better.

111. a. Either my brothers or my best friend are dropping by to help. (1:05)
    b. Either my brothers or my best friend is dropping by to help.
    c. I don't know which one is better.

112. a. Several of our employee's mothers will be at the reception. (12:04)
    b. Several of our employees' mothers will be at the reception.
    c. I don't know which one is better.

113. a. The new drafting tables are five feet long and four feet wide. (9:06)
    b. The new drafting tables are five ft. long and four ft. wide.
    c. I don't know which one is better.

114. a. When Logan retired, she left the east coast and moved out west. (6:06)
    b. When Logan retired, she left the East Coast and moved out West.
    c. I don't know which one is better.

115. a. The parking-lot attendant asked for our voucher. (15:15)
    b. The parking lot attendant asked for our voucher.
    c. I don't know which one is better.

116. a. We really got a good price this time. (13:25)
    b. They gave us a good price this time.
    c. I don't know which one is better.

117. a. I bought me a new suit for the interview. (2:05)
    b. I bought myself a new suit for the interview.
    c. I don't know which one is better.

118. a. <u>Everyone involved gives</u> her credit for saving the company. (17:05)
    b. <u>She is given</u> credit for saving the company.
    c. I don't know which one is better.

119. a. That painting on the wall <u>surely</u> is interesting. (13:26)
    b. That painting on the wall <u>sure</u> is interesting.
    c. I don't know which one is better.

120. a. The shipment arrived around <u>August 15, 1978</u>. (7:12)
    b. The shipment arrived around the <u>15th of August, 1978</u>.
    c. I don't know which one is better.

121. a. If you will drive faster, <u>we might</u> be there by dinnertime. (16:09)
    b. If you will drive faster, we <u>might could</u> be there by dinnertime.
    c. I don't know which one is better.

122. a. That report comes out at the <u>end of the month</u>. (15:16)
    b. That report comes out at the <u>end-of-the-month</u>.
    c. I don't know which one is better.

123. a. A lar<u>ge,</u> weather map covered the wall. (3:14)
    b. A large weather map covered the wall.
    c. I don't know which one is better.

124. a. Every Sunday afternoon, she <u>lays</u> out by the pool. (13:28)
    b. Every Sunday afternoon, she <u>lies</u> out by the pool.
    c. I don't know which one is better.

125. a. This year they took <u>seperate</u> vacations. (14:10)
    b. This year they took <u>separate</u> vacations.
    c. I don't know which one is better.

126. a. Send these brochures to <u>whoever</u> writes for information. (8:09)
    b. Send these brochures to <u>whomever</u> writes for information.
    c. I don't know which one is better.

127. a. The director and <u>myself</u> decided to offer you the promotion. (2:05 and 18:16)
    b. The director and <u>I</u> decided to offer you the promotion.
    c. I don't know which one is better.

128. a. By December, she had made a <u>20-percent</u> return on the investment. (15:17)
    b. By December, she had made a <u>20 percent</u> return on the investment.
    c. I don't know which one is better.

129. a. I know nothing about ar<u>t,</u> nevertheless, I spent two days in the Louvre. (4:08)
    b. I know nothing about ar<u>t;</u> nevertheless, I spent two days in the Louvre.
    c. I don't know which one is better.

130. a. I <u>set</u> the box on your back porch last week. (13:29)
    b. I <u>sat</u> the box on your back porch last week.
    c. I don't know which one is better.

131. a. To <u>de-emphasize</u> information, place it in a short, simple sentence. (19:05)
    b. To <u>emphasize</u> information, place it in a short, simple sentence.
    c. I don't know which one is more nearly true.

English for Professionals **137**

132. a. We all feel <u>bad</u> about the mistake. (13:09 and 18:17)
     b. We all feel <u>badly</u> about the mistake.
     c. I don't know which one is better.

133. a. Roses, tulips, and irises—<u>these flowers were his favorites</u>. (5:09-10)
     b. Roses, tulips, and irises—<u>were his favorite flowers</u>.
     c. I don't know which one is better.

134. a. We accept shipments through both <u>ports of entry</u>. (11:12)
     b. We accept shipments through both <u>port of entries</u>.
     c. I don't know which one is better.

135. a. Sarah is out of tow<u>n; c</u>onsequently, the meeting will be postponed. (4:09)
     b. Sarah is out of tow<u>n. C</u>onsequently, the meeting will be postponed.
     c. I don't know which one is better.

136. a. <u>Parents</u> should never place <u>their</u> children in a military school. (18:18)
     b. <u>One</u> should never place <u>one's</u> children in a military school.
     c. I don't know which one is better.

137. a. Paul fixed <u>himself</u> a sandwich and left. (2:06)
     b. Paul fixed <u>hisself</u> a sandwich and left.
     c. I don't know which one is better.

138. a. <u>Their</u> going to reach Denver by midnight. (14:11)
     b. <u>They're</u> going to reach Denver by midnight.
     c. I don't know which one is better.

139. a. These plates are <u>rounder</u> than the others. (10:08)
     b. These plates are <u>more nearly round</u> than the others.
     c. I don't know which one is better.

140. a. They arrived in New York on <u>January 20th</u>. (7:12-13)
     b. They arrived in New York on <u>the 20th of January</u>.
     c. I don't know which one is better.

141. a. She <u>posited</u> <u>myriad</u> <u>constructs</u> for the <u>deterioration</u> of our <u>profit margin</u>. (18:21)
     b. She <u>suggested</u> <u>several</u> possible <u>causes</u> for the <u>decline</u> in <u>our profits</u>.
     c. I don't know which one is better.

142. a. Mark Nevill<u>e, </u>our newest employe<u>e, </u>has a degree from Stanford. (3:16)
     b. Mark Neville our newest employee has a degree from Stanford.
     c. I don't know which one is better.

143. a. **Placing information in a one-sentence paragraph <u>emphasizes</u> it.** (19:06)
     b. **Placing information in a one-sentence paragraph <u>de-emphasizes</u> it.**
     c. I don't know which one is more nearly true.

144. a. All the <u>childrens'</u> toys have been put away. (12:03)
     b. All the <u>children's</u> toys have been put away.
     c. I don't know which one is better.

145. a. She asked an officer at First National whether the <u>b</u>ank will back us. (6:07)
     b. She asked an officer at First National whether the <u>B</u>ank will back us.
     c. I don't know which one is better.

146. a. If we <u>word process</u> the report, we can easily revise it. (18:22)
     b. If we <u>write the report on a word processor</u>, we can easily revise it.
     c. I don't know which one is better.

147. a. On the right side of the car <u>stand</u> the three people who went with me. (1:06)
     b. On the right side of the car <u>stands</u> the three people who went with me.
     c. I don't know which one is better.

148. a. She is <u>to</u> busy to answer the phone. (14:12)
     b. She is <u>too</u> busy to answer the phone.
     c. I don't know which one is better.

149. a. She bought them at a <u>20%</u> discount. (9:07)
     b. She bought them at a <u>20 percent</u> discount.
     c. I don't know which one is better.

150. a. If I <u>had had</u> more courage, we wouldn't be in this fix. (16:10)
     b. If I <u>had shown</u> more courage, we wouldn't be in this fix.
     c. I don't know which one is better.

151. a. The cleaning crew will be here until <u>12 midnight</u>. (7:16)
     b. The cleaning crew will be here until <u>12 AM</u>.
     c. I don't know which one is better.

152. a. They prepared <u>theirselves</u> for a serious confrontation. (2:06)
     b. They prepared <u>themselves</u> for a serious confrontation.
     c. I don't know which one is better.

153. a. The word from the <u>h</u>ill (Capitol Hill) is that the bill will pass. (6:09)
     b. The word from the <u>H</u>ill (Capitol Hill) is that the bill will pass.
     c. I don't know which one is better.

154. a. **Good business letters <u>should seldom</u> be more than one page long.** (18:26)
     b. **<u>Nothing is wrong</u> with business letters that are more than one page long.**
     c. I don't know which one is more nearly true.

155. a. We appreciate <u>your</u> taking the time to help. (2:07)
     b. We appreciate <u>you</u> taking the time to help.
     c. I don't know which one is better.

156. a. Someon<u>e's</u> car was parked too close to ours. (12:04)
     b. Someon<u>es</u> car was parked too close to ours.
     c. I don't know which one is better.

157. a. The meeting will start at <u>1:00</u> PM. (7:18)
     b. The meeting will start at <u>1</u> PM.
     c. I don't know which one is better.

158. a. She injured two of the verte<u>bras</u> in her lower back. (11:13)
     b. She injured two of the verte<u>brae</u> in her lower back.
     c. I don't know which one is better.

159. a. The cement now <u>costs</u> twice as much as it did last year. (1:07)
     b. The cement now <u>cost</u> twice as much as it did last year.
     c. I don't know which one is better.

English for Professionals 139

160. a. She is the woman <u>whom we hired</u> to take David Baty's position. (8:12)
    b. She is the woman <u>we hired</u> to take David Baty's position.
    c. I don't know which one is better.

161. **a. Good sentence variety calls for a few <u>short</u> sentences mixed with numerous <u>long</u> sentences. (18:28)**
    b. Good sentence variety calls for a few <u>long</u> sentences mixed with numerous <u>short</u> sentences.
    c. I don't know which one is more nearly true.

162. a. We expect a load of <u>frieght</u> tomorrow morning. (14:13)
    b. We expect a load of <u>freight</u> tomorrow morning.
    c. I don't know which one is better.

163. a. <u>Fred's</u> winning the lottery changed everything. (2:08)
    b. <u>Fred</u> winning the lottery changed everything.
    c. I don't know which one is better.

164. a. The computer costs about <u>a thousand dollars</u>. (7:19)
    b. The computer costs about <u>$1,000</u>.
    c. I don't know which one is better.

165. a. Our <u>P</u>ersonnel <u>D</u>ivision is working with their <u>T</u>raining <u>D</u>epartment. (6:10)
    b. Our <u>p</u>ersonnel <u>d</u>ivision is working with their <u>t</u>raining <u>d</u>epartment.
    c. I don't know which one is better.

166. **a. A letter that requires <u>several commas</u> probably uses better sentence variety than one that needs no commas. (18:29)**
    b. A letter that requires <u>no commas</u> probably uses better sentence variety than one that uses several commas.
    c. I don't know which one is more nearly true.

167. a. How many CEO<u>s</u> will attend? (9:09)
    b. How many CEO<u>'s</u> will attend?
    c. I don't know which one is better.

168. **a. Specific language <u>emphasizes</u> information. (19:07)**
    b. Specific language <u>de-emphasizes</u> information.
    c. I don't know which one is more nearly true.

169. a. Yesterday I talked to Judy Norflee<u>t, o</u>ur representative in Richmond. (3:17)
    b. Yesterday I talked to Judy Norflee<u>t o</u>ur representative in Richmond.
    c. I don't know which one is better.

170. a. When we tried to change his mind, he was <u>immovable</u>. (14:14)
    b. When we tried to change his mind, he was <u>immoveable</u>.
    c. I don't know which one is better.

171. a. This year the budget will exceed <u>$3 billion</u>. (7:20)
    b. This year the budget will exceed <u>$3,000,000,000</u>.
    c. I don't know which one is better.

172. a. He is the <u>most kindest</u> person I know. (10:09)
    b. He is the <u>kindest</u> person I know.
    c. I don't know which one is better.

173. a. Their county receives extensive support from federal agencies. (6:11)
     b. Their county receives extensive support from Federal agencies.
     c. I don't know which one is better.

174. a. Them computers won't do the job. (2:10)
     b. Those computers won't do the job.
     c. I don't know which one is better.

175. a. **Clichés have little impact on your reader and should be avoided.** (18:31)
     b. **Business and legal clichés help establish a writer's professionalism.**
     c. I don't know which one is more nearly true.

176. a. Not one of them brought their notes along. (2:11)
     b. Not one of them brought his notes along.
     c. I don't know which one is better.

177. a. We will meet in Office Tower II. (6:12)
     b. We will meet in office tower II.
     c. I don't know which one is better.

178. a. In our society today, the importance of paper can hardly be exaggerated. (18:32)
     b. In our society, the importance of paper can hardly be exaggerated.
     c. I don't know which one is better.

179. a. The conference will be held in Room 105. (6:12)
     b. The conference will be held in room 105.
     c. I don't know which one is better.

180. a. The gift cost $10.00, but he spent $18.50 on the postage. (7:21)
     b. The gift cost $10, but he spent $18.50 on the postage.
     c. I don't know which one is better.

181. a. Caring for Your Pool: Two New Ideas (a title) (6:13)
     b. Caring for your Pool: Two new Ideas (a title)
     c. I don't know which one is better.

182. a. **Items listed in a column are emphasized when they are numbered or when bullets are placed in front of them.** (19:08)
     b. **Items listed in a column are de-emphasized when they are numbered or when bullets are placed in front of them.**
     c. I don't know which one is more nearly true.

183. a. Our community has thousands of dollars invested in the project. (7:22)
     b. Our community has $1000s invested in the project.
     c. I don't know which one is better.

184. a. Someone should bring a calculator along. (2:11)
     b. Someone should bring their calculator along.
     c. I don't know which one is better.

185. a. Give this packet to the person she hires. (8:12)
     b. Give this packet to whomever she hires.
     c. I don't know which one is better.

English for Professionals 141

186. a. <u>If</u> the loan is approved, <u>then</u> we can start construction. (18:33)
    b. <u>If</u> the loan is approved, we can start construction.
    c. I don't know which one is better.

187. a. Jane and Steve had a contest to see which one can proofread <u>fastest</u>. (10:10)
    b. Jane and Steve had a contest to see which one can proofread <u>faster</u>.
    c. I don't know which one is better.

188. a. Each telephone call from the room adds <u>50 cents</u> to the bill. (7:23)
    b. Each telephone call from the room adds <u>50¢</u> to the bill.
    c. I don't know which one is better.

189. a. They discussed the contract. The<u>n, </u>they toured the plant. (4:10)
    b. They discussed the contract. Then they toured the plant.
    c. I don't know which one is better.

190. a. Their bid <u>toped</u> ours by $5000. (14:15)
    b. Their bid <u>topped</u> ours by $5000.
    c. I don't know which one is better.

191. a. The campaign started on July 20, 1990 and ended a month later. (3:19)
    b. The campaign started on July 20, 199<u>0, </u>and ended a month later.
    c. I don't know which one is better.

192. a. <u>A staff meeting was called by the head of our department</u>. (17:04-06)
    b. <u>The head of our department called a staff meeting</u>.
    c. I don't know which one is better.

193. a. The light bulbs were <u>75 cents</u> each, but the switch cost $4.98. (7:24)
    b. The light bulbs were <u>$.75</u> each, but the switch cost $4.98.
    c. I don't know which one is better.

194. a. Her son graduated from college when he was <u>sixteen-years-old</u>. (15:18)
    b. Her son graduated from college when he was <u>sixteen years old</u>.
    c. I don't know which one is better.

195. a. He sent <u>John's and Mary's</u> report to the front office. (12:13)
    b. He sent <u>John and Mary's</u> report to the front office.
    c. I don't know which one is better.

196. a. The report was mailed on Wednesda<u>y, </u>December 17, 1947. (3:20)
    b. The report was mailed on Wednesday December 17, 1947.
    c. I don't know which one is better.

197. a. The woman who repaired your car is <u>well trained</u>. (15:19)
    b. The woman who repaired your car is <u>well-trained</u>.
    c. I don't know which one is better.

198. a. We sold about <u>6000</u> of those trucks at $22,000 each. (7:25)
    b. We sold about <u>6,000</u> of those trucks at $22,000 each.
    c. I don't know which one is better.

199. a. Waco, Texas is her favorite city. (3:23)
    b. Waco, Texa<u>s, </u>is her favorite city.
    c. I don't know which one is better.

200. a. We all agreed that it was an unusual <u>occurence</u>. (14:16)
     b. We all agreed that it was an unusual <u>occurrence</u>.
     c. I don't know which one is better.

201. a. **A letter with <u>plenty of white space</u> is easier to read.** (18:36)
     b. **A letter with <u>minimal white space</u> is easier to read.**
     c. I don't know which one is more nearly true.

202. a. When she said, "I love Pari<u>s", </u>I relaxed. (3:24)
     b. When she said, "I love Pari<u>s."</u> I relaxed.
     c. I don't know which one is better.

203. a. We could <u>of</u> danced all night. (16:08)
     b. We could <u>have</u> danced all night.
     c. I don't know which one is better.

204. a. Fewer than <u>0.5</u> percent of American families own one. (7:26)
     b. Fewer than <u>.5</u> percent of American families own one.
     c. I don't know which one is better.

205. a. Those particular records are <u>nonessential</u>. (15:24)
     b. Those particular records are <u>non-essential</u>.
     c. I don't know which one is better.

206. a. She was a child of the <u>60's</u>. (7:27)
     b. She was a child of the <u>60s</u>.
     c. I don't know which one is better.

ANSWERS TO THE PRETEST

These answers are arranged by chapter, not by numerical order. The numbers in parentheses identify the sections that explain each item.

FOLLOW THESE INSTRUCTIONS CAREFULLY! Circle each item that you missed or answered with a *c*. ***Circle them on these pages, not on the answer sheet.***

When you are through checking your answers, you will see where your major and minor weaknesses lie. The numbers in parentheses will help you develop the skills you need without spending hours reading about things you already know.

1 SUBJECT-VERB AGREEMENT

14. a (1:02)   44. b (1:03)   83. b (1:04)   111. b (1:05)   147. a (1:06)   159. a (1:07)

2 PRONOUNS

10. b (2:02)   36. a (2:02)   53. b (2:02)   71. b (2:03)   91. a (2:04)   104. b (2:04)   117. b (2:05)
127. b (2:05)   137. a (2:06)   152. b (2:06)   155. a (2:07)   163. a (2:08)   174. b (2:10)   176. a (2:11)
184. a (2:11)

3 FOUR COMMA RULES

6. b (3:02)   11. b (3:02)   28. a (3:04)   39. a (3:06)   48. a (3:06)   58. a (3:07)   75. b (3:09)   88. a (3:10)
96. b (3:11-12)   107. a (3:13)   123. b (3:14)   142. a (3:16)   169. a (3:17)   191. b (3:19)   196. a (3:20)
199. b (3:23)   202. b (3:24)

4 THE SEMICOLON

22. a (4:03)   80. b (4:07)   129. b (4:08)   135. b (4:09)   189. b (4:10)

5 COLONS AND DASHES

2. a (5:02)   18. b (5:03)   64. a (5:05)   82. a (5:05)   100. a (5:06)   133. a (5:09-10)

6 CAPITALIZATION

8. b (6:03)   32. a (6:02)   50. b (6:04)   67. b (6:05)   114. b (6:06)   145. a (6:07)   153. b (6:09)
165. a (6:10)   173. a (6:11)   177. a (6:12)   179. a (6:12)   181. a (6:13)

7 NUMBERS

1. b (7:02)   5. b (7:02)   26. a (7:05)   34. a (7:03)   56. a (7:06)   69. a (7:08)   84. a (7:07)   106. a (7:09)
120. a (7:12)   140. b (7:12-13)   151. a (7:16)   157. b (7:18)   164. b (7:19)   171. a (7:20)   180. b (7:21)
183. a (7:22)   188. a (7:23)   193. b (7:24)   198. b (7:25)   204. a (7:26)   206. b (7:27)

8 WHO OR WHOM, WHOEVER OR WHOMEVER

30. a (8:02)   61. a (8:04)   65. b (8:04)   76. b (8:05)   94. b (8:06-07)   98. a (8:08)   126. a (8:09)
160. b (8:11)   185. a (8:12)

9 ABBREVIATIONS

51. b (9:03)   113. a (9:06)   149. b (9:07)   167. a (9:09)

Chapter 9 covers more material than these items reflect.

10 COMPARATIVES AND SUPERLATIVES

43. a (10:02)   90. a (10:04)   109. a (10:06)   139. b (10:08)   172. b (10:09)   187. b (10:10)

11 PLURALS

16. a (11:04)   41. b (11:06)   47. b (11:07)   73. b (11:10)   134. a (11:12)   158. b (11:13)

12 POSSESSIVES

20. b (12:03)   38. a (12:10)   93. a (12:12)   112. b (12:04)   144. b (12:03)   156. a (12:04)   195. b (12:13)

13 FREQUENTLY MISUSED WORDS

7. a (13:02)   13. b (13:02)   21. a (13:03)   27. a (13:05)   29. a (13:06)   31. b (13:07)   40. a (13:08)
45. b (13:08)   52. b (13:10)   54. b (13:11)   57. a (13:12)   63. b (13:13)   66. b (13:16)   68. b (13:27)
74. a (13:14)   78. b (13:17)   86. b (13:18)   92. b (13:19)   95. a (13:20)   97. a (13:21)   99. b (13:22)
101. a (13:23)   103. b (13:24)   108. a (13:24)   116. b (13:25)   119. a (13:26)   124. b (13:28)   130. a (13:29)
132. a (13:09)

14 SPELLING

9. b (14:03)   23. a (14:04)   35. b (14:05)   55. b (14:06)   70. a (14:07)   89. b (14:08)   102. a (14:09)
125. b (14:10)   138. b (14:11)   148. b (14:12)   162. b (14:13)   170. a (14:14)   190. b (14:15)
200. b (14:16)

Chapter 14 covers more material than these items reflect.

15 HYPHENATING COMPOUND ADJECTIVES

3. a (15:09)   19. b (15:08)   37. a (15:10)   46. a (15:12)   60. a (15:11)   79. b (15:13)   85. a (15:14)
115. b (15:15)   122. a (15:16)   128. b (15:17)   194. b (15:18)   197. a (15:19)   205. a (15:24)

16 THE SUBJUNCTIVE

81. a (16:07)   121. a (16:09)   150. b (16:10)   203. b (16:08)

Chapter 16 covers more material than these items reflect.

17 ACTIVE VOICE VERSUS PASSIVE VOICE

25. a (17:04)   118. b (17:05)   192. b (17:04-06)

Chapter 17 covers more material than these items reflect.

English for Professionals

18 THE BUSINESS STYLE: SIMPLE CLARITY

4. b (18:02)   12. b (18:03)   17. a (18:04)   24. a (18:05)   25. a (18:19)   33. a (18:06)   42. b (18:08)
49. a (18:09)   62. b (18:10)   68. b (18:11)   77. a (18:12)   87. a (18:13)   105. b (18:14)   110. b (18:15)
127. b (18:16)   132. a (18:17)   136. a (18:18)   141. b (18:21)   146. b (18:22)   154. a (18:26)   161. b (18:28)
166. a (18:29)   175. a (18:31)   178. b (18:32)   186. b (18:33)   201. a (18:36)

19 EMPHASIZING IMPORTANT INFORMATION

15. a (19:02)   59. b (19:03)   72. a (19:04)   131. b (19:05)   143. a (19:06)   168. a (19:07)   182. a (19:08)

20 ORGANIZING LETTERS

This pretest can't evaluate your ability to organize business letters.

21 SPECIAL LETTERS

This pretest can't evaluate your ability to write good job applications (résumé cover letters), interview follow-up notes, recommendations, resignations, dismissals, congratulatory notes, and thank-you notes.

22 PROOFREADING SKILLS

This pretest can't evaluate your proofreading skills.

23 IMPROVING YOUR ENGLISH

The information in this chapter is not the type of material that can be included in a pretest.

24 REFERENCE BOOKS

The information in this chapter is not the type of material that can be included in a pretest.

APPENDIX B: ANSWERS TO THE EXERCISES

1 SUBJECT-VERB AGREEMENT

Page 2

PRACTICE 1-B (The subjects are underlined. The verbs are italicized.)

1. steps *collapsed*
2. Someone *wrote*
3. You (understood) *forget*
4. cousin *is*
5. CEO *is*
6. train *will be*
7. assistant *needs*
8. Jeff *feels*
9. Glenda and Roy *will be married*
10. She *owns and manages*
11. train *is*
12. woman *lives*
13. You (understood) *ask*
14. They *are going to announce*
15. car *was parked*

Page 3

PRACTICE 1-D

1. type *is*   2. team *was*   3. flight *was*

PRACTICE 1-E

1. food *is*   tables *are*   2. parts *were*   work *has*   3. tickets *are*   space *is*

Page 4

PRACTICE 1-F

1. bacteria *are*   2. parenthesis *prints*   3. nuclei *were*

PRACTICE 1-G

1. Carol nor her brothers *want*

2. the backpacks or the canoe *is*

3. the company cars nor one of the company trucks *was* ("Of the company trucks" is a prepositional phrase.)

Page 5

PRACTICE 1-H

1. people *were*   2. badger *lives*   3. bricks *are*

PRACTICE 1-I

1. brother *fasts*   2. ledger *lists*   3. plan *consists*

Page 5

EXERCISE 1, SUBJECT-VERB AGREEMENT

1. <u>data</u> *are*   2. <u>book</u> *is*   3. <u>variables</u> *are*   4. <u>eagle</u> *nests*   5. <u>size</u> *is*   6. <u>foundation</u> *lies*   7. <u>trash</u> *comes*

Page 6

8. <u>media</u> *are*   9. Enough of <u>us</u> *were* ("Enough" can be singular or plural.)   10. <u>collection</u> *is*

11. <u>group</u> *is*   12. <u>assortment</u> *is*   13. <u>alumnus</u> *is*   14. <u>house</u> *costs*   15. <u>vertebra</u> *was*   16. <u>doll</u> *sits*

17. <u>paint</u> *has*   18. <u>A lot of fungi</u> *are* ("A lot" can be singular or plural.)   19. <u>group</u> *is*   20. <u>type</u> *is*

21. <u>potential</u> *is*   22. <u>syllabi</u> *were*   23. <u>discussion</u> *is*   24. <u>reasons</u> *are*   25. <u>news</u> *is*

26. <u>coach</u> *contests*   27. <u>violinists</u> *want*   28. <u>cacti</u> *are*   29. <u>boats</u> *are*   30. <u>tree</u> *casts*   31. <u>sisters</u> *have*

32. <u>batch</u> *looks*   33. <u>suspect</u> *insists*   34. <u>flock</u> *has*   35. <u>nuclei</u> *have*

2 PRONOUNS

Page 7

PRACTICE 2-A

1. Karl and **she** live . . . .   2. Are you and **he** looking . . . .

3. Sonia and **I** will ride with **her** and Bill.

Page 8

PRACTICE 2-B

1. . . . than **he** (can).   2. . . . as **she** (was)   3. . . . than **he** (is)

PRACTICE 2-C

1. The Queen sent Robert and **me** . . . .   2. He hurt **himself** . . . .   3. . . . I wrote **myself** . . . .

Page 9

PRACTICE 2-D

1. **Their** flying to Vancouver . . . .   2. We admire **his** kicking the ball . . . .

3. **Your** agreeing to come . . . .

PRACTICE 2-E

1. Those (or These) trucks are ready to roll.

2. Why won't you let those (or these) kids ride the pony?

Page 10

PRACTICE 2-F

a. *Anyone* is singular. *Them*, *they*, and *their* are all plural. These words should all be singular or all be plural.

b. If anyone calls, tell **him he** can leave **his** message with Sue.

b. If anyone calls, tell **him or her he or she** can leave **his or her** message with Sue.

c. If **people** (one possibility) call, tell **them they** can leave **their** message with Sue.

d. If anyone calls, tell Sue to take a message (one possibility).

English for Professionals

Page 11
EXERCISE 2, PRONOUNS
I.
1. she (can) 2. me 3. my 4. myself 5. those she (was) 6. him 7. their 8. himself 9. Bill and I 10. His 11. me 12. I (am) 13. your 14. we (are) 15. she 16. she (is) 17. him 18. she 19. your 20. he (can) 21. me 22. he Joe and me 23. Those themselves 24. Their 25. He she Roger and me

Page 12
II.
1. a. *Everyone* is singular and *their* is plural. Both should be singular or both should be plural.
   b. Everyone remembered to bring **his** checkbook.
   c. Everyone remembered to bring **his or her** checkbook.
   d. **All** of them remembered to bring **their** checkbooks.
   e. Everyone remembered to bring **a** checkbook.

2. a. *A Nurse* is singular while *they* is plural. Both should be singular or both should be plural.
   b. A nurse can make more money if **he** works weekends. (Some people would chose *she* because most nurses are females, but **he** can be used because both males and females serve as nurses.)
   c. A nurse can make more money if **he or she** works weekends.
   d. **Nurses** can make more money if **they** work weekends.
   e. A nurse can make more money **by working weekends**. (one possibility)

3. a. *One* is singular while *they* is plural. Both should be singular or both should be plural.
   b. Not one of the employees was stopped if **he** was wearing **his** photo ID.
   c. Not one of the employees was stopped if **he or she** was wearing **his or her** photo ID.
   d. **None** of the employees (one possibility) were stopped if **they** were wearing **their** photo IDs.
   e. Not one of the employees **wearing a photo ID** was stopped (one possibility).

3 FOUR COMMA RULES
Page 13
PRACTICE 3-A
1. They processed your order today, so you should receive it by Monday.
2. The interstates are almost impassable, and the airport is closed due to high winds, so our auditor might not be here tomorrow.

Page 14
3. Bill cut the wood, (optional) and Mary loaded it.
4. Add milk and butter to the flour, but don't add salt at this point.
5. no commas

Page 15
PRACTICE 3-B
1. If the storm strikes during the night, they won't stand a chance.
2. Her mind stopped wandering as soon as the nurse called her name (no commas).
3. Coughing and wheezing, (optional) the child trailed after his mother.
4. On the road to Zanzibar, she made her fortune and lost her soul.
5. In the Outback, (optional) sheep are the key to survival.
6. After four days of hard work, they cleared the old mine shaft, (Rule One) and with cheers and shouting all around, he was taken to the hospital.

Page 16
PRACTICE 3-C
1. She chopped the onions, peeled the potatoes, and carefully added the spices.
2. The computer is too old, the room needs to be painted, and the rent is a bit high.
3. A deck of cards, a bottle, a bath a week, and freedom from labor were all he ever wanted.
4. In January, April, July, and October, (Rule Two) new quarterly reports will be issued.
5. He ran a small, unprofitable business for two years, fought as a mercenary for one year, and spent the rest of his short, turbulent life taming crocodiles.

Page 17
PRACTICE 3-D
1. Little Patsy, who had never been to town before, followed her brother everywhere.
2. Computers, unlike people, are fast and accurate.
3. Lee Howard talked to Sid Norman, our vice president, and solved the problem.
4. Her accounts are with the oldest bank in town, Planters' Trust.
5. When we ordered the book, the one he recommended, (Rules Two and Four) we also bought a new pen

PRACTICE 3-E
1. He reached Lima on December 28, 1942, and crossed into Colombia the following Sunday, January 3, 1943.
2. He reached Lima on 15 December 1942 and crossed into Colombia the following Sunday, 3 January 1943.
3. We drove to Augusta, Maine, in June 1984 to check on our investments.

Page 19
EXERCISE 3a, COMMAS
1. Darryl helped Jose write a résumé , (1) and Joyce helped him compose the cover letter.
2. The van was rented this morning, (1) and the pickup truck is in the shop, (1) but we still have several station wagons.
3. Sheila arrived this morning, (optional 1) but Steve flew in yesterday.
4. Take good notes, (1) and let me know whether the new program will affect our division's responsibilities.
5. Dorothy completed the letter by noon and mailed it during her lunch break (no commas).
6. They leased more office space so that they could hire six new employees (no commas).
7. We left an hour early so we wouldn't have to deal with rush hour traffic (no commas).
8. She didn't sign out, (1) so she must still be in the immediate area.
9. In order to keep his appointment, (2) he left for work an hour early.
10. We must purchase three printers, (1) but if they offer us a professional discount, (2) we will go ahead and order five.
11. Within one hour, (optional 2) we had interviewed four applicants.
12. We worked all weekend, (1) and by Monday morning, (optional 2) the report was in the mail.
13. We need to add envelopes, (3) labels, (3) and pens to the shopping list.
14. They want to read your analysis, (3) study the contract, (3) and review our proposals before they schedule a meeting.
15. The desks are in the warehouse, (3) the chairs are on the truck, (3) and the mattresses are on the loading dock.
16. A tall, (3) well-dressed woman met us at the door.

English for Professionals 151

17. Our last mail clerk, (4) the one you met at the reception, (4) was promoted and was transferred to Palo Alto, (4) California.
18. Our office has a new computer, (4) the very model you recommended.
19. The auction started at 9 AM on Tuesday, (4) May 10, (4) 1995, (4) and ended the following Wednesday afternoon.
20. If the lawyers, (3) the accountants, (3) and the labor leaders can work out the agreement, (2) we will start production by the end of the year.
21. Most of our money is in mutual funds (no commas).

Page 20

22. Our division managers, (4) including Dorothy, (3) Charlie, (3) and Lee, (4) are eager to work out a simple, (3) effective compromise.
23. Payroll taxes, (3) income taxes, (3) and users' fees have reduced our income, (1) so we must find a way to operate more profitably.
24. In some cases, (optional 2) we work directly with the manufacturers, (1) but most of the time, (optional 2) we have to go through wholesale dealers.
25. By the time we had completed our long, (3) exhaustive study, (2) we knew we had to cut costs, (3) expand operations, (3) or find new markets.
26. Their briefing on advances in computer technology, (4) the one you heard in Boston, (4) was well planned, (3) well presented, (3) and highly informative.
27. The steel beams are in place, (1) but without the safety belts, (4) the ones OSHA requires, (2&4) we can't continue working.
28. The business he founded as a young man made him a millionaire and allowed him to pay for the education of all four of his children and all ten of his grandchildren (no commas).
29. Sometimes, (optional 2) the well-drilling equipment breaks down, (1) and on those occasions, (optional 2) we call Crossville, (4) Pennsylvania, (4) to order parts.
30. When they bought the new hard drive for the computer, (4) the PC in Shirley's office, (2&4) they should have bought a new printer, (3) a new monitor, (3) and a new keyboard.
31. If the invoice arrives, (optional 2) send me a copy of it, (1) and tell the supervisor in the warehouse to treat the shipment with care.
32. He sent me a short, (3) well-written memorandum dealing with two important topics, (4) employee morale and continuing education.
33. We signed a four-year contract. (no commas)
34. Our counterparts in France have requested that we try to work out a simple method for keeping them supplied with raw materials and equipment so that they can avoid costly shutdowns and layoffs (no commas).
35. Punctuation skills, (4) like math skills, (4) are developed through long, (3) repetitive drills, (1) and with patience, (optional 2) anyone can learn to punctuate correctly.

Page 21
EXERCISE 3b, COMMAS
1. If the weather is warm enough, (2) he wears T-shirts to work.
2. Richard replaced a knob, (3) adjusted the fine tuning, (3) and tightened two nuts.
3. In spite of the loud, (3) banging noises, (2) they slept, (1) but none of them slept well.
4. Gail hung the curtains, (1) and with the help of friends, (2) we moved the sofa in.
5. Monday, (optional 2) my uncle, (4) the one who lives uptown, (4) came by to see us.
6. Charles will leave next Thursday, (4) March 15.
7. Margaret spoke with the members of the board three days before she decided to announce her resignation to the public (no commas).
8. We can order now, (optional 1) or we can wait.

152   *CommonSense Grammar and Style*

9. Occasionally, (optional 2) <u>Ms. Collins</u>, (4) our night dispatcher, (4) <u>works the morning shift</u>.
10. <u>They completed the house</u>, (1) yet <u>the final project</u>, (4) the landscaping, (4) <u>had to be postponed</u>.
11. Whenever he came to town, (2) <u>he stopped for coffee at the Colonial Inn</u>.
12. <u>We worked all day on the budget but could not come up with the money for a new computer</u> (no commas).
13. <u>We have similar goals</u>, (1) so <u>you don't have to worry about cooperation</u>.
14. Though she had never been on a horse, (2) <u>she dressed, (3) cursed, (3) and drank like a cowhand</u>.
15. When the auditor found two serious, (3) perplexing discrepancies, (2) <u>we had to revise our procedures</u>.
16. <u>Our buyer is in Salem, (4) Massachusetts, (4) for a show</u>, (1) and <u>the manager is in Seattle, (4) Washington, (4) attending a conference</u>, (1) but <u>the manager's assistant will be glad to talk to you</u>.
17. After a short stint in the Army, (4) however, (2 & 4) <u>he took a job with the CIA</u>.
18. <u>Show her the program documentation</u>, (1) but <u>don't let her enter the computer center</u>.
19. By noon, (optional 2) <u>they were in Chicago</u>, (1) but <u>no one was there to meet them</u>.
20. <u>The treaty was signed on 31 March 1992</u>, (1) and as you can see, (optional 2) <u>we all live in peace</u>.
21. <u>The trucks, (3) materials, (3) and crews are ready</u>, (1) so <u>we should start work tomorrow</u>.

Page 22
22. <u>He won the battle</u>, (optional 1) but <u>she won the war</u>.
23. <u>She left Brussels, (4) Belgium, (4) on December 14, (4) 1956</u>.
24. <u>A technician from the computer shop on Third and Walnut repaired my computer so that it now works as well as a new one</u> (no commas).
25. <u>Wait for gold prices to drop</u>, (1) and <u>invest your excess cash in mutual funds</u>.
26. When Sue went to Europe, (2) <u>Carla, (3) Norma, (3) and Pam</u>, (4) her three best friends, (4) <u>traveled with her</u>.
27. Back then, (optional 2) <u>the demand for plastics was limited</u>, (1) so <u>profits were low</u>, (1) but now, (optional 2) <u>we can't keep up with the orders</u>.
28. When I talked to Bill, (4) our contact in Reno, (2 & 4) <u>he said Alfred is at fault</u>, (1) but <u>I think Carol Smothers</u>, (4) their assistant, (4) <u>mailed us the wrong bill</u>.
29. In spite of the confusion, (2) <u>the students, (3) the faculty, (3) and the administrators met</u>, (1) and <u>the conflicts</u>, (4) at least the critical ones, (4) <u>were resolved</u>.
30. When we ask him to write letters, (3) run errands, (3) or file, (2) <u>he acts as if he is being rewarded</u>.
31. Sometimes, (optional 2) <u>she feels left out</u>, (4) especially when we go to lunch without her.
32. Although she graduated, (optional 2) <u>she never looked for a job</u>, (1) and <u>her grandparents, (3) parents, (3) and brothers still support her</u>.
33. <u>The lights in the work area must be replaced</u> because they are too intense and create unnecessary eye fatigue (no commas).
34. Although Katharine was new, (optional 2) <u>her supervisor</u>, (4) the chief accountant, (4) <u>trained her well</u>, (1) and after only two weeks, (optional 2) <u>she felt like an experienced employee</u>.
35. <u>That big, (3) mean, (3) ugly Hell's Angel is Carol's date</u>, (1) and <u>her rich, (3) stuffy father is upset</u>.

Page 23
EXERCISE 3c, COMMAS
1. If you want to write better letters, (2) <u>learn to proofread carefully</u>.
2. <u>He was brilliant</u>, (1) but without a dictionary, (2 optional) <u>he couldn't spell his own name</u>.
3. In terms of structure, (optional 2) <u>passive voice and active voice are completely different</u>.
4. <u>Capitalization can be tricky</u>, (1) but if you proofread carefully and follow a few simple guidelines, (2) <u>you will seldom make errors</u>.
5. Years ago, (optional 2) <u>stilted phrases</u>, (4) fancy words with little meaning, (4) <u>were commonly used in business writing</u>.
6. <u>The most important "special letter" is the letter of application</u> (no commas).

English for Professionals

7. Letters of recommendation are also extremely important because you could slow the advancement of a friend's career if you don't know how to write a good one (no commas).
8. Specific language emphasizes information, (optional 1) but general language de-emphasizes it.
9. Occasionally, (optional 2) the bad news, (4) the statement of refusal, (4) should be in the opening sentence.
10. Euphemisms can help us deal with painful or distasteful matters, (1) but clichés , (4) overworked words and phrases, (4) interfere with communication.
11. When your letter must say *NO*, (2) try to write it without saying *NO*, (1) and always maintain respect for your reader.
12. Goofy reading, (4) pronouncing each syllable with the same dull tone, (4) is an excellent way to proofread.
13. *Fowler* is an excellent book on usage and is now available in paperback (no commas).
14. Do not apologize for saying *NO*, (4) not unless the problem is your fault.
15. Since most people mispronounce prerogative, (2) they also misspell it.
16. Roger will drive, (optional 1) and Sharon will take notes.
17. After she practiced using lie and lay for two weeks, (2) she began to choose the correct word unconsciously.
18. Use active voice most of the time, (1) and try to avoid noun piles.
19. To defend his position, (optional 2) he hid behind company policy, (1) and his letter was a flop.

Page 24

20. Ain't is nonstandard English, (1) and if you keep using it, (2) you could hurt your chances for a successful career.
21. The reals, (3) gets, (3) and verys have been cleaned out, (1) so the language in our report sounds much fresher.
22. She wrote the letter so that he could concentrate on his report (no commas).
23. He did it (no commas).
24. Mr. D. R. Swanson met with the president this afternoon and agreed to write the guidelines that will describe our company's preferred formats for letters and memorandums (no commas).
25. Write him another letter saying *NO*, (1) and this time, (optional 2) use the direct approach.
26. When closing a bad-news letter, (2) use resale, (3) offer an alternative, (3) refer confidently to future business relations, (3) or take more than one of these approaches.
27. If you have to deny credit, (4) however, (2 & 4) do your best to keep the applicant as a cash customer, (1) and eventually, (optional 2) that person could become a trusted client.
28. Rule One commas are easy to use, (1) and Rules Three and Four seldom cause trouble, (1) but Rule Two commas cause more problems than all the others combined.
29. In spite of the mistake, (2) the manager, (3) the clerk, (3) and he behaved like gentlemen, (1) and they solved their problems, (4) at least the important ones.
30. When a group of words can stand alone as a simple sentence, (2) it's called an independent clause.
31. The fastest way to proofread effectively is to combine two strategies, (4) goofy reading and reading with a straightedge.
32. Although she wrote several letters of application, (2) she did a sloppy job, (1) and neither CBS, (3) NBC, (3) nor ABC invited her in for an interview.
33. Semicolons may be used in complex sentences to replace certain commas but are not commonly used to separate independent clauses or to add afterthoughts (no commas).
34. He wrote a short, (3) polite letter with good word variety, (3) good sentence variety, (3) and plenty of white space.
35. In spite of her lack of experience, (2) Jane, (4) the owner's daughter, (4) was given the job, (1) but after only two weeks, (optional 2) she resigned and eagerly returned to college.

4 THE SEMICOLON

Page 26

EXERCISE 4, SEMICOLONS

1. Howard, the junior partner, will be in charge; but he won't make any major decisions. (Most good business writers would replace the semicolon with a comma.)
2. They have lived in Pueblo, Colorado; Santa Fe, New Mexico; and El Paso, Texas.
   (Most good business writers would keep these semicolons.)
3. Sarah thought we were upset with her; on the contrary, we think she has made excellent progress. (Most good business writers would use a period and capitalize On.)
4. Ms. Simms is highly competitive; I'm not. (Most good business writers would use a period.)
5. We didn't expect to win all of our games; however, we did expect to win the tournament. (Most good business writers would use a period and capitalize However.)
6. Commodities prices are rising rapidly; for example, the last two weeks have seen the price of wheat increase more than 30 percent.
   (Most good business writers would use a period and capitalize For.)
7. Before he applied to IBM, he took his civil service exam; and he seriously considered a career with the Department of Labor, the Department of Commerce, or the FBI.
   (Most good business writers would replace the semicolon with a comma.)
8. The training sessions are scheduled for Tuesday, November 6; Thursday, November 15; and Monday, December 3. (Most good business writers would keep these semicolons.)
9. They bought their farm several years before Honda picked the site for a plant; then they sold it for a considerable profit. (Most good business writers would use a period and capitalize Then. Do not place a comma after Then.)
10. She invited Gil, Sandra, George, and Sam; and Ralph invited me. (Under ordinary circumstances, most good business writers would use a comma instead of a semicolon. Here, however, the semicolon makes the sentence more readable and could be the best punctuation mark.
    If you would like to avoid the semicolon, use a period, and start the next sentence with Ralph. You could also use a period and capitalize And, but most conservative writers would object.)

5 COLONS AND DASHES

Page 28

EXERCISE 5, COLONS AND DASHES

1. They furnished all of the wood: the logs, the beams, and the studs.
2. The company will pay most of your expenses: for example, food, travel, and lodging.
3. Cathy Gomez, Sally Berk, and Alice Jenkins—each of these employees deserve our deep appreciation.
4. With your claim, please submit the following documentation:
   Your preapproved authorization to travel
   Your meal receipts
   Your mileage records
5. With your claim, please submit your:
   Travel voucher
   Meal receipts
   Mileage records
6. When you turn in your claim, please:
   Submit your travel log.
   Turn in your expense records.
   Sign the travel voucher.

English for Professionals

7. Correct.
8. Don't forget to bring the eating utensils: the knives, the forks, and the spoons.
9. Typing, taking dictation, and answering the phone—those tasks occupy most of an administrative assistant's day.
10. Correct.
11. She has several assets: namely, intelligence, perseverance, and an understanding manner.

6 CAPITALIZATION

Page 30

EXERCISE 6, CAPITALIZATION

I.
1. Chamber of Commerce . . . fair   2. North   3. federal government . . . House   4. Chief Justice
5. mother . . . Uncle   6. congresswomen . . . Sunbelt . . . Senator
7. Vice President . . . Personnel Division   8. head . . . Finance Department . . . Gulf   9. none

II.
Cutting the Water Off: A Trip up and Back down the Dow Jones Average
Open Communications: A Study of Self-Esteem

7 NUMBERS

Page 34

EXERCISE 7, NUMBERS

I.
1. On the 30th of January (or January 30), they decided to sell all five computers for about $13,000.
2. She called at 12 noon and came over around 3 PM.
3. The report indicates that one-fourth of their employees earn more than $20 an hour.
4. The pens cost $.65 each, and the pads cost $1.25 each.
5. The car costs $22,000 new, but a two-year-old model sells for about $8,000.
6. The sausages average about 0.55 pounds each.
7. Place the order after the 3d of March (or March 3 or 3 March) but before the 4th of April (or April 4 or 4 April).
8. Nineteen people at the meeting invested several thousand dollars in the project (or Of those people attending the meeting, 19 invested several thousand dollars in the project).
9. In 1803, Robert Livingston bought 530 million acres for a little over $27 million.
10. Americans like to brag that Livingston paid only 3 cents (or $.03) an acre for the Louisiana Purchase, but the actual price was about 5 cents (or $.05) an acre.
11. Carlos Lopez, aged 42, is in charge of all three divisions.
12. By noon yesterday, 7 doctors and 12 nurses volunteered.
13. The state's budget deficit exceeded $2¼ billion (or $2.25 billion).
14. In 1882, on the 22d of September (or September 22 or 22 September), his great-grandmother was born in Norway.
15. Hundreds of our investors earned thousands of dollars in the '70s.

II.
Printing the brochures cost a few hundred dollars more at PrintCo, but they delivered them by 12 noon on the 18th of August (or August 18 or 18 August), and we had them in the mail 14 days early. We sent out around 12,000 brochures, and they generated $15,945 in profit.

8 WHO OR WHOM, WHOEVER OR WHOMEVER

Page 35
PRACTICE 8-B

1 through 10, whom

Page 36
PRACTICE 8-C

1. whom (He must defeat *him* [or *her* or *them*] to become champion.)
2. who (*He* [or *she* or *they*] was your opponent.)
3. whom (You will pick up *him* [or *her* or *them*] on your way to work.)
4. who (*He* [or *she* or *they*] started the move to increase profits.)
5. whom (You will be meeting *him* [or *her* or *them*] at the conference.)
6. who (*He* [or *she* or *they*] was her best friend in college.)
7. whom (We will take *him* [or *her* or *them*] to the club tonight.)
8. who (*He* [or *she* or *they*] carried out the board's orders.)
9. whom (They elected *him* [or *her* or *them*] to serve as chairperson.)
10. who (*He* [or *she* or *they*] asked for the assignment first.)

Page 37
PRACTICE 8-D

1. who (*He* [or *she* or *they*] took first place at Daytona.)
2. whom (We promoted *him* [or *her* or *them*].)
3. whom (You read the book to *him* [or *her* or *them*].)
4. who (*He* [or *she* or *they*] finishes last.)
5. whom (You saw *him* [or *her* or *them*] on TV.)
6. who drove the car (*He* [or *she* or *they*] drove the car.)
7. who was honored at the banquet (*He* [or *she* or *they*] was honored at the banquet.)
8. who moved to Australia (*He* [or *she* or *they*] moved to Australia.)
9. whom you investigated (You investigated *him* [or *her* or *them*].)
10. who had the neatest résumé (*He* [or *she* or *they*] had the neatest résumé.)
11. who she believes are deserving (She believes *he* [or *she* or *they*] is deserving.)

Page 38
12. whom they prefer (They prefer *him* [or *her* or *them*].)
13. whom they gave the records to (They gave the records to *him* [or *her* or *them*].)
14. who achieved the goal (*He* [or *she* or *they*] achieved the goal.)
15. who it was (*Was* is a form of *to be*.)

Can any of the *whom*s be dropped? Yes, all of them.

PRACTICE 8-E

1. who they are (*Are* is a form of *to be*.)
2. who the new president will be (*Will be* is a form of *to be*.)
3. Whom (She was looking for *him* [or *her* or *them*].) (*Was looking* is a form of *to look*, not of *to be*.)
4. who the embezzler might have been (*Might have been* is a form of *to be*.)
5. who the executor is (*Is* is a form of *to be*.)

Page 39
PRACTICE 8-F

1. whomever (You want *him* [or *her* or *them*].)
2. Whomever (You invite *him* [or *her* or *them*].)

English for Professionals

3. Whoever (*He* [or *she* or *they*] angers her.)
4. whoever (*He* [or *she* or *they*] works in her division.)
5. whoever (He thinks *he* [or *she* or *they*] is corrupt.)
6. whomever we can find with the proper credentials (We can find *him* [or *her* or *them*].)
7. whoever lives in her area (*He* [or *she* or *they*] lives in her area.)
8. Whomever we ask to speak (We ask *him* [or *her* or *them*] to speak.)
9. whomever she has an account with (She has an account with *him* [or *her* or *them*].)
10. whoever is on the phone (*He* [or *she* or *they*] is on the phone.)

Can any of the *whom*s be dropped? Yes, all of them. (We don't want to drop the *who*s.)

Page 40
EXERCISE 8a, WHO OR WHOM, WHOEVER OR WHOMEVER
1. Who (*He* [or *she* or *they*] is the best choice for mayor.)
2. Whom (She has been talking to *him* [or *her* or *them*].)
3. who writes the fastest (*He* [or *she* or *they*] writes the fastest.)
4. whoever needed it (*He* [or *she* or *they*] needed it.)
5. who the suspect is (*Is* is a form of *to be*.)
6. whom we will be sending to California (We will be sending *him* [or *her* or *them*] to California.)
7. who work in the computer center now (*He* [or *she* or *they*] works in the computer center now.)
8. whoever is willing to back him (*He* [or *she* or *they*] is willing to back him.)
9. whom it was designed for (It was designed for *him* [or *her* or *them*].)
10. whom the director chose for the parts (The director chose *him* [or *her* or *them*] for the parts.)
11. who the winner will be (*Will be* is a form of *to be*.)
12. whom (You bought your car from *him* [or *her* or *them*].)
13. whoever works with the word processor (*He* [or *she* or *they*] works with the word processor.)
14. who she thought were qualified (She thought *he* [or *she* or *they*] was qualified.)
15. who accumulated the most overtime (*He* [or *she* or *they*] accumulated the most overtime.)
16. whomever they send to work with us (They send *him* [or *her* or *them*] to work with us.)
17. Whom (They will leave their children with *him* [or *her* or *them*].)
18. who worked for you last summer (*He* [or *she* or *they*] worked for you last summer.)
19. whomever we send (We send *him* [or *her* or *them*].)
20. whom Ms. Jenkins had helped before (Ms. Jenkins had helped *him* [or *her* or *them*]before.)
21. Whoever the best candidate might have been (*Might have been* is a form of *to be*.)
22. whoever is in charge of production (*He* [or *she* or *they*] is in charge of production.)
23. whom (You worked under *him* [or *her* or *them*].)
24. Whom (You buried *him* [or *her* or *them*] in the basement.)

Page 41
25. Who (*They* are the people primarily responsible for the audits.)
26. Whomever you pick (You pick *him* [or *her* or *them*].)
27. whoever attended the party (*He* [or *she* or *they*] attended the party.)
28. Whom (She interviewed *him* [or *her* or *them*] this morning.)
29. who won the contest (*He* [or *she* or *they*] won the contest.)
30. whoever he assumes will back us (He assumes *he* [or *she* or *they*] will back us.)
31. whoever is willing to sign the receipt (*He* [or *she* or *they*] is willing to sign the receipt.)
32. who was appointed to fill Joe's seat (*He* [or *she* or *they*] was appointed to fill Joe's seat.)
33. whom (You ordered parts from *him* [or *her* or *them*].)
34. who it was (*Was* is a form of *to be.*)
    who wrote the letter (*He* [or *she* or *they*] wrote the letter.)
35. whomever they recommend (They recommend *him* [or *her* or *them*].)

Can any of the *whom*s be dropped? Yes, in sentences 6, 9, 10, and 20.

Can any of the *whomever*s be changed to *anyone* or *the person*? Yes, in sentences 16, 19, 26, and 35.

Do any of the *whom*s resist being dropped? Yes, in sentences 2, 12, 17, 23, 24, 28, and 33. Notice that they are all questions and that they all ask for a person's name.

Do any of the *whomever*s resist being changed to *anyone* or *the person*? No.

Page 42

EXERCISE 8b, AVOIDING *WHOM* AND *WHOMEVER*

1. He will vote for anyone she nominates.
2. He is one of the children we wrote letters to.
3. This *whom* is probably unavoidable.
4. Drop *whom*.
5. The young woman will have to marry anyone (*or* the man) her father selects.
6. Who sent you the telegram? (one possibility)
7. Drop *whom*.
8. Anyone they send will be able to handle the job.
9. Drop *whom*.
10. This *whom* is probably unavoidable.
11. Drop *whom*.
12. This *whom* is probably unavoidable.
13. We send free samples to anyone she puts on the list.
14. Drop *whom*.
15. Anyone they select (*or* The person they select) as judge must be fully qualified.

9 ABBREVIATIONS

Page 44

EXERCISE 9, ABBREVIATIONS

I.

1. William R. Cook Jr will be our new company president.
2. They had to hire two CPAs to take her place.
3. When he hit the ice, he locked the brakes and slid about 100 feet.
4. American Mining Corp (only if the company writes it that way) is one of the most prosperous corporations in our area.
5. Correct.
6. About 60 percent of the employees will attend the party, and the number one attraction will be Mr. Williams' magic show.
7. She ordered four of them at $5 each.
8. Our daughter is a junior in high school.
9. He must have taken his management courses around 1000 BC.
10. Their CEO's computer is being repaired.

II.

The SBOPs (Standard Base Operating Procedures) or Standard Base Operating Procedures (SBOPs) require citizens of the USA and Canada to obtain written permission from the commanding officer before entering the base. Officials of the Kentucky and Tennessee governments need only sign in at the gate. Sundays through Fridays, all civilian visitors must be off base by 11 PM.

English for Professionals 159

10 COMPARATIVES AND SUPERLATIVES

Page 46

EXERCISE 10a, COMPARATIVES AND SUPERLATIVES

1. shorter, shortest   2. more wonderful, most wonderful   3. more playful, most playful

4. more, most   5. shallower, shallowest or more shallow, most shallow

6. more nearly plumb, most nearly plumb   7. more quickly, most quickly

EXERCISE 10b, COMPARATIVES AND SUPERLATIVES

1. Brian is the *better* of their two first-team linebackers.

2. She's the nicest person I know. (Drop *most*.)

3. No logical solution. A person is either pregnant or not pregnant.

11 PLURALS

Page 47

PRACTICE 11-A

1. boxes   2. Nashes   3. Huffines   4. gases (or gasses)   5. Jacobs

Page 48

PRACTICE 11-B

1. folksingers   2. casts   3. quarries   4. portfolios   5. chambers of commerce   6. concertos

7. sisters-in-law   8. attorneys

Page 49

EXERCISE 11, FORMING PLURALS

1. cameos   2. attorneys general   3. oxen   4. Betsy Rosses   5. steamships   6. buoys

7. men-of-war   8 tomatoes   9. axes   10. X rays   11. cacti   12. wrists

13. Summers (Summerses is unlikely.)   14. micros   15. juries   16. daughters-in-law

17. parentheses   18. Baggins (Bagginses is unlikely.)   19. masts   20. Stutz (or Stutzes)

12 POSSESSIVES

Page 51

PRACTICE 12-A

1. Street's (plurals = parks)   2. Brothers' (plurals = brothers, paintings)

3. program's (plural = instructions)   4. babies' (plurals = babies, tests)

5. president's (plurals = we, plans, us)   6. man's (plural = none)

7. mother-in-law's (plural = offices)   8. nurses' (plural = clinics, nurses, schedules)

9. attorney general's (plural = decisions)   10. box's (plurals = contents, secrets)

Page 52

PRACTICE 12-B

1. children's (plurals = they, children, playrooms)   2. Ms. Moyers' (plurals = none)

3. chests of drawers' (plural = drawers)   4. criteria's (plurals = criteria)

5. sons-in-law's (plurals = sons-in-law, parents)

PRACTICE 12-C

1. everyone's (plural = interests)   2. no one's (plural = opinions)
3. somebody's (plurals = loans, assets)   4. anyone's (plurals = meetings, they)
5. nobody's (plural = checks)

Page 53
PRACTICE 12-D

1. its (plural = repairs)   2. hers (plural = books)   3. whose (plurals = contracts, bids)
4. his (plural = notes)   5. theirs (plurals = visual aids, slides)

PRACTICE 12-E

1. Mr. Sturgis's   2. witness's   3. Los Angeles's   4. Mr. Ross's   5. Congress's

Page 54
PRACTICE 12-F

1. Steve and Carol's   2. Ms. Roy and Mr. Hamilton's   3. his and her   4. Sears, IBM, and Intel's

PRACTICE 12-G

1. Ms. Hamrix'   2. Valázquez'   3. Dr Stutz' (or Dr Stutz's)

Page 55
EXERCISE 12a, FORMING POSSESSIVES

1. girl's   2. its   3. buses'   4. couch's   5. Mr. Rodriguez'   6. dogs'   7. no one's   8. your
9. fox's   10. media's   11. Richard's   12. Mr. Crow and Ms. Lee's   13. His and her
14. Smithsons'   15. ours   16. bush's   17. everyone's   18. mice's   19. whose
20. daughter-in-law's   21. mine   22. whoever   23. Homo sapiens'   24. men's   25. pens'
Page 56
26. someone's   27. Ms. Lipschutz'   28. Sue and Charlie's   29. his and her (or her and his)
30. cacti's   31. Mr. Maddox'   32. Ms. Dobbins'   33. stories'   34. anyone's   35. her
36. printers'   37. oxen's   38. whose   39. school's   40. films'

EXERCISE 12b, APOSTROPHES AND POSSESSIVES

The *novel's* main character is Huckleberry Finn. *It's* Huck and *Jim's* ambition to escape civilization and its laws. *It's* the *widow's* ambition to subject them to society and its rules. The *river's* promise is freedom, so Huck and Jim, *civilization's* victims, flee on its untamed currents. Each time they go ashore, the runaways are faced with *society's* ridiculous, cruel, or pathetic behavior, but the *runaways'* refuge is always the savage river. The *nation's* hypocrisy and greed, her *citizens'* inhumanity to man are more terrifying than the cold, blind forces of primeval nature.

13 FREQUENTLY MISUSED WORDS
Page 62
PRACTICE 13-A

1. lay   2. set   3. lying   4. set   5. lie
Page 63
6. laid   7. lying   8. lie   9. sat   10. laid   11. sat   12. laying   13. set   14. lay   15. setting

EXERCISE 13, FREQUENTLY MISUSED WORDS

1. Most   2. consensus   3. lies   4. assured   5. May   already
6. (Avoid *real*, *really*, and *very*. Drop them or use fresher words.)   people   7. set   8. lent   averages
9. anyone   every day   10. any one   everyday   11. farther   12. lain   13. fewer
14. with   from   15. Regardless   16. sits   17. surely   18. between   19. principal   20. sitting

Page 64

21. number   22. amount   23. a   that   24. principles   25. lies   26. ensure or insure   27. person
28. principal   29. set   30. effect   31. Every one   32. Everyone   33. lying   34. lending
35. among   36. further   37. affected   38. a   an   a
39. bought (Avoid *real*, really, and *very*. Drop them or use fresher words.)   40. principal
41. each other   42. insure   43. one another   44. effect   45. effect   46. unprincipled
47. which   surely   48. already   49. lay   50. bad

14 SPELLING

Page 68

EXERCISE 14, SPELLING

II

1. A   2. C   3. A   4. B   5. C   6. C   7. B   8. C   9. B   10. exception to A   11. A
12. C   13. A   14. C   15. A   16. B   17. exception to A   18. B   19. A   20. C   21. A
22. C   23. B   24. C   25. exception to B

15 HYPHENATING COMPOUND ADJECTIVES

Page 69

PRACTICE 15-A

1. mean   new
2. part-time   other
3. well-dressed   iron
4. lucky   50-foot

Page 71

PRACTICE 15-B

1. mean   2. part-time   3. high-strung   4. lucky   5. none

Page 72

PRACTICE 15-C

1. blue-green   2. three- to five-day   3. all-female   4. well-dressed, self-confident

PRACTICE 15-D

1. blue-green   2. first-rate   3. all-female   4. even-tempered

Page 74

PRACTICE 15-E

1. Five-year, 4 percent = exception 5
2. income-producing, income tax = exception 3
3. well-designed ("*Well-built*" is not in *Merriam-Webster*.)

162   *CommonSense Grammar and Style*

4. day-to-day, made to order = exception 4
5. old-world, new book's = exception 2
6. tax-exempt, desperately needed = exception 1
7. 6-foot-long, 12 feet long = exception 6
8. self-made, self-conscious
9. hard-won, well-known ("*Well-known*" is in *Merriam-Webster*.)

Page 75

EXERCISE 15, HYPHENATING COMPOUND ADJECTIVES

1. two-year, 4 percent
2. handmade chess set (Surprise! *Handmade* has evolved into one word. *Chess set* is a two- word noun.)
3. Three well-known
4. self-conscious   light-headed
5. up-to-date   up to date
6. nonsmoker,   prenuptial (*Non-* and *pre-* are prefixes that are not ordinarily hyphenated.)
7. first-come, first-served
8. maintenance workers'   well?understood ("*Well-understood*" is not in *Merriam-Webster*.)
9. corporate financial advisor (*Financial advisor* is a two-word noun.)   tax-deductible.
10. 50-, 75-, and 100-foot   five years
11. worn-out   20- or 25-year   12 percent
12. three-layered   New Year's Eve
13. ill-advised personnel policies   well?balanced ("*Well-balanced*" is in *Merriam-Webster*.)   self-esteem
14. self-respecting   high-spirited
15. well?designed ("*Well-designed*" is not in *Merriam-Webster*.)   highly qualified
16. carefully written   new employee's
17. well-known   ex-mother-in-law   self-employed   interior decorating
18. foreign-born   end of the month

Page 76

19. 8 percent   cost-effective
20. seven-day-a-week, around-the-clock   three months
21. ill?tempered ("*Ill-tempered*" is in *Merriam-Webster*.)   highly respected
22. informal support group (*Support group* is a two-word noun.)   ill?advised ("Ill-advised" is in *Merriam-Webster*.)
23. makeshift (Surprise! *Makeshift* has evolved into a single word.)   high- and low-range
24. long-lost   Nobel Prize-winning
25. brightly painted   customized hot rod (*Hot rod* is a two-word noun.)
26. civil service   word processing
27. young well digger   favorite side dish
28. community-based   newfound (*Newfound* has evolved into a single word.)
29. five- and six-year-olds   ill?prepared ("*Ill-prepared*" is not in *Merriam-Webster*.)
30. well-planned   six hours
31. self-educated   0.8 percent
32. cautiously constructed   native-born
33. old car's   out of commission
34. commonsense (*Common sense* is a two-word noun, but [surprise!] it has evolved into a one-word adjective.) ready-made
35. out-of-control   out of control

English for Professionals

36. three days   high-   and low-tech
37. antidefamation   midwinter (*Anti-* and *mid-* are prefixes that are not ordinarily hyphenated.)
38. ill-gotten gains are ill?deserved ("*Ill-deserved*" is not in *Merriam-Webster*.)
39. so-called   ten-year   eight years
40. elegantly dressed   Georgia Tech
41. well-nourished   young man's
42. computer-driven   self-addressed
43. easygoing (Surprise! *Easygoing* has evolved into one word.)   sweat-stained
44. propane- and diesel-filled   new storage facility (*Storage facility* is a two-word noun.)
45. high school   three-hour-long
46. ex-director   well?equipped ("*Well-equipped*" is not in *Merriam-Webster*.)   self-assured
47. heavily wooded   ill-constructed
48. steel-reinforced   70 percent
49. Last year's   40 pages
50. twenty-year-old   well-heeled real estate agent   second- and third-floor apartments self-igniting cost-of-living

16 THE SUBJUNCTIVE
Page 79
PRACTICE 16-A
1. . . . if her car were not running well?   2. If he were here, ...   3. I wish you were . . . .
4. If the wind were stronger, ...   5. . . . if she were trained in surveying.
6. "I wish I were a teddy bear."

PRACTICE 16-B
1. . . . I might have been of assistance.   2. She could have stayed longer . . . .
3. . . . they would have had plenty to eat.

Page 80
PRACTICE 16-C
. . , we might have seen Tom.   . . ,we could have seen Tom.   . . , we would have seen Tom.

PRACTICE 16-D
1. . . . if he had hired a better campaign manager (one possibility).
2. If we had brought more money with us, . . . (one possibility).
3. . . . if she had worn a feather in her ear (one possibility).

Page 81
EXERCISE 16, THE SUBJUNCTIVE
I.
1. If they had been given less help, . . . (one possibility).
2. . . . he would have done his share of the work.
3. . . . maybe you could (you could, you might) attend night school.
4. If Ernestine were in charge, ...
5. If the cabinet had been designed with more compartments, . . . (one possibility).
6. I wish I were in London . . . .
7. He could have worked all day . . . .
8. . . . if the company had used more effective accounting procedures (one possibility).

9. . . . maybe he could (he could, he might) move to Hawaii.
10. Mark might have won the race if he had worn better shoes (one possibility).

II.
1. I wish I were as strong as Superman.
2. If I were as strong as Superman, I could leap tall buildings.
3. If you had been there, we would have played pinochle all day.
4. I wish Ramona were as busy now as she was last year.
5. If Roy and Dale were here, they would not let Snidely McWhiplash evict us.

17 ACTIVE VOICE VERSUS PASSIVE VOICE
Page 86
EXERCISE 17, ACTIVE VOICE VERSUS PASSIVE VOICE

I.
1. A presentation on office layouts was given by Mary Carter.
2. The report was turned out by our new printer in record time.
3. Our old printer has been repaired by someone.
4. Better looking reports are turned out by the old printer than by the new one.
5. The crew was given credit for saving our lives by the passengers, the press, and airport officials.

Number 3 (Our old printer has been repaired) is better in passive voice if *by someone* is dropped because we don't know or care who the *DOER* is.

Number 5 (The crew was given credit for saving our lives) is better in passive voice if "the passengers, press, and airport officials" is dropped because the *DOER* is a large, diverse group.

II.
1. The director scheduled a meeting for employees interested in college classes.
2. Jane wrote the report and Wanda edited it.
3. Someone (one possibility) has painted our house.
4. Someone (one possibility) delivered the chair last Friday.
5. Thomas Jefferson wrote the Constitution in 1787.

Numbers 3 and 4 work better in passive voice because we don't know, and probably don't care, who these *DOER*s are.

Number 5 could work either way, depending on our center of interest. If the date is of primary importance, the sentence can be left in passive voice. If the *DOER* is critical, it should be expressed in active voice.

III.
The grievance committee has prepared a bulletin concerning employees smoking in the halls. Some nonsmokers are raising objections to the smoke. If employees can't find a solution to the problem, the president could outlaw all smoking. Concerned employees need to submit suggestions so a compromise can be reached. (48 words)

Most people would agree that the passage in active voice is clearer.

Once the paragraph is in active voice, the need for further simplification is obvious.

The grievance committee has prepared a bulletin about smoking in the halls. Some nonsmokers object to the smoke. If employees can't solve the problem, the president could outlaw all smoking. Please submit your suggestions so a compromise can be reached. (39 words, one possibility)

"So a compromise can be reached" is best left in passive voice because the *DOER* is a large, diverse group.

English for Professionals 165

18 THE BUSINESS STYLE: SIMPLE CLARITY
Page 96
TOPICS FOR DISCUSSION
1. Answers vary.
2. Many reasons could be given. Perhaps the most obvious is that the private business sector can't afford the irritation, confusion, and inefficiency that go with bureaucratic gobbledygook. Their customers would go elsewhere.
3. Many creative writers subscribe to the principles of simple clarity.
4. Yes. Human beings tend to be self-centered, and we overuse those pronouns.
5. People who rarely use *real(ly)*, *very*, and *get* often have above average vocabularies and express themselves well.
6. They are uninviting and difficult to read.
7. Answers vary.
8. Answers vary.

EXERCISE 18, CLARITY
1. A. It is too long or wordy (18:04). It uses *and/or* (18:10).
   B. Ms. Howard wants us to convince the contractors that they should let us move in before the parking lot and landscaping are complete (one possibility).
2. A. It uses the pompous (and incorrect) *myself* (18:16). ***Corporate vehicles inspection procedures*** is a noun pile (18:14).
   B. Mr. Van Buren and I will be in charge of the procedures for inspecting our corporation's vehicles (one possibility).
3. A. It uses medical jargon (18:08). ***Physician*** is repeated unnecessarily (18:30).
   B. My doctor said I have a cold and nasal congestion, and he told me to take aspirin and stay in bed (one possibility).

Page 97
4. A. It uses *very* (18:35). ***By the president*** and ***by the company*** indicate passive voice (18:19).
   B. The president has reached an important decision concerning the annual bonuses our company pays (one possibility).
5. A. It uses recipe English (18:20).
   B. Open the valve in the line that feeds the pump. Then turn the pump on (one possibility).
6. A. It uses *yours truly* to avoid the pronoun *I* (18:02). It uses *shall* (18:13).
   B. I will be in your office by midafternoon (one possibility).
7. A. It uses the / (18:10) and is vague because it avoids the pronoun *you* (18:03).
   B. Please complete the report and distribute it by the end of the month (one possibility). (The *you* is understood in this case.)
8. A. It uses *one* (18:18). It uses *get* (18:35). ***If–then*** is redundant (18:33).
   B. Anyone who has the opportunity should invest in high-yield bonds (one possibility).
9. A. ***The author of this letter*** is used to avoid I (18:02). ***Servicing*** is an uncommon verb built from a common noun (18:22).
   B. As your factory representative, *I* am deeply committed to customer ***service*** (one possibility).

Page 98
10. A. It is vague because it avoids the pronoun *you* (18:03). ***Desired*** is an uncommon word in this situation. (18:21).
    B. Before you select an option from the main menu, key in your password, and press ENTER (one possibility).

11. A. *Badly* should be *bad* (18:17). It uses *really* (18:35). It uses *myself* incorrectly (pompous) (18:16).
    B. Senator Fogbound felt bad about the mistake and extended a heartfelt apology to William and me (one possibility).
12. A. It uses a triple redundancy (*the reason why is because*) (18:32).
    B. She came to see Mike.
13. A. It uses *which* unnecessarily (18:12). It is vague because it avoids the pronoun you (18:03).
    B. Today, you should assign the passwords our users need to access the mainframe (one possibility).
14. A. *This* is a dangling demonstrative pronoun (18:15). *Only designed* is unclear (18:25).
    B. This engine is designed to burn only diesel fuel (one possibility).
15. A. *Enclosed please find* is a cliché (18:31). It uses *which* unnecessarily (18:12). *So kindly* is a cliché (18:31). *Make further inquiry pertaining to* is uncommon language (18:21). It uses *shall* (18:13). It uses *get* (18:35). *Without further delay* is a cliché (18:31).
    B. Here is the résumé you requested. If you would like to review my references or examine my professional credentials, I can send them to you right away (one possibility).

19 EMPHASIZING IMPORTANT INFORMATION
Page 100
TOPICS FOR DISCUSSION
1. When everything is emphasized, nothing is emphasized.
2. Answers vary.
3. Answers vary.
4. Answers vary.
5. When you know the person well, and a friendly, informal atmosphere has been established (one possible answer).

Page 101
EXERCISE 19, EMPHASIS
1. B (It uses bold print.)   2. B (It uses short, simple sentences.)   3. B (It uses specific language, but it's rude. Emphasis is not always positive.)   4. A (It uses an indented block.)   5. B (It uses capital letters.)   6. A (It underlines the information.)
Page 102
7. B (It uses a column and bullets.)   8. A (It states that the information is important and says why it's important.)   9. B (It uses a one-sentence paragraph.)   10. A (It places the information at the beginning of the letter.)

20 ORGANIZING LETTERS
Page 109
TOPICS FOR DISCUSSION
1. Yes
2. Yes
3. Answers vary. Yes, when your reader needs to know you are hesitant.
4. Answers vary. Yes, when you have decided to avoid dealing with that person ever again.
5. Too many people think familiarity cancels the need for courtesy. It does not.
6. Memorandums stay within a company. The people who write them are more likely to know one another well and have probably established mutual respect.

English for Professionals

7. The paragraph that presents the bad news should be long so the bad news can be placed in the middle and thus be de-emphasized
8. Answers vary. Yes, the indirect approach could be used to enhance a pleasant surprise.
9. Answers vary. As a matter of courtesy, you might explain, telling your reader why the matter is illegal or unethical, and then say *NO*.
10. Answers vary.
11. Answers vary.
12. Answers vary. Yes, businesses must compete for customers, but government bureaucracies are usually monopolies.
13. None

Page 110
EXERCISE 20, LETTERS
Each letter and each memorandum must be judged individually according to the principles taught in this chapter.

21 SPECIAL LETTERS
Page 118
TOPICS FOR DISCUSSION
1. Answers vary.
2. Answers vary. A supervisor who can't support deserving employees could, in turn, lose their support.
3. You could be sued.
4. Answers vary.
5. Answers vary.

EXERCISE 21, SPECIAL LETTERS
1 and 2, Answers vary.
3 and 4, The letters must be evaluated individually according to the principles taught in this chapter.

23 IMPROVING YOUR ENGLISH
Page 122
TOPICS FOR DISCUSSION
1. through 4. Answers vary.
5. A dialect is one of various types of English and is distinguished by unique elements of vocabulary, pronunciation, and usage. Dialects are usually associated with a specific geographic region.

For example, our "Southern dialect" is more properly called the "Scotch-Irish" dialect because settlers from Northern Ireland brought it to this country. The people of Northern Ireland are largely of Scottish origin, so their dialect is called Scotch-Irish.

24 REFERENCE BOOKS

Page 124

TOPICS FOR DISCUSSION

1. Modern dictionaries are the products of a tradition that Samuel Johnson started in England around 1755. The first American dictionary appeared in 1828 when Noah Webster published his revision of Johnson's dictionary. Today numerous excellent dictionaries are on the market.

   No single dictionary is the official American dictionary, but ***Merriam-Webster's Collegiate Dictionary*** and its big brother, ***Webster's Third New International Dictionary***, are widely accepted as the leaders.

   The editors of dictionaries are not the ones who decide what constitutes standard English. Instead, they draw their standards from, as Noah Webster put it, "the enlightened members of each community." For example, if you want to know whether you should use the word *data* as a singular or as a plural noun, don't ask a computer programmer. Check to see how prominent scientists, writers, and educators use it.

2. It's the most thorough of English dictionaries. The 1989 edition has 12 volumes and sells for $2778.

3. Answers vary.

INDEX

a—an, 13:02
a lot
    singular or plural, 1:03
    spelling, 14:03
Abbreviations, 9:01-11
    acceptable use of, 9:01-08
    periods with, 9:11
    plurals, 9:09
    possessives, 9:10
    symbols, 9:07
    with people's names, 9:04-05
Academic style, page ii, 3:12, 7:01, 18:01-07, 18:18, 18:37, 24:08
Acronyms, 9:03
Active voice, 17:01-02, 17:04, 17:06-07, 18:19
Adverbial conjunctions (see Conjunctive adverbs)
Adjectives
    commas with, 3:13-14, 3:27
    comparatives and superlatives, 10:02-05, 10:07-10
    complement, 15:01, 15:03-06, 15:12, 15:16, 15:19
    compound, 15:01-22
    hyphenated, 15:01-22
    with noun piles, 18:14
    predicate, 15:03
Adverbs, comparative and superlative, 10:06
affect—effect, 13:03-04
ain't, 2:10, 13:16, 14:02, 14:18, 18:34
all, singular or plural, 1:03
all right, 14:04
Alliteration, 18:15
already, 13:16
alumni—alumnus, 1:04
AM and PM, 7:16-17
The American Heritage Dictionary of the English Language, 24:03
among, 13:10
amount—number, 13:05
an, 13:02
and/or, 18:10
Anglo-Saxon, 14:01
any, singular or plural, 1:03
anyone—any one, 13:07 Apologizing, 20:19

Apostrophes (see also Possessives), 7:27
Applications for employment, 21:02-08
Approximations
    money, 7:19, 9:07
    numbers, 7:02, 7:08
assure—ensure—insure, 13:08
bad—badly, 13:09, 18:17
Bad-news letters, 19:11, 20:11-26
between—among, 13:10
Bold print, 6:17, 19:10
Bureaucratic English (see Gobbledygook)
Business style, 18:01-37
    avoiding pomposity, 18:08-24
    avoiding restraints of academic English, 18:02-07
    being rude, 20:26
by, 17:03, 17:06-07, 22;02
can—may, 13:12
cannot, 14:06
Capitalization, 6:01-17
    buildings, 6:12
    with colons in titles, 6:14
    in columns, 5:04
    companies and organizations, 6:07
    departments and divisions, 6:10
    for emphasis, 19:10
    federal, 6:11
    headings, 6:13-16
    with hyphens in titles, 6:15
    memorandum subject lines, 6:13
    nicknames of organizations, 6:09
    personal titles and positions, 6:02-05
    rooms, 6:12
    shortened geographic names, 6:06
    titles, 6:13-17
Cents and the cent symbol, 7:23-24
Cities, punctuation with, 3:23
Clarity, 4:11, 4:13, 17:07, 18:01-37,
Clichés, 17:07, 18:31, 20:05, 21:08
Colons, 5:01-07
    and capitalization in titles, 6:14
    introducing lists, 5:02-03
    introducing lists in columns, 5:04-06
    and logic (parallelism), 5:07

Colons, continued
   with quotation marks, 3:26
Columns, 5:04-07
   capitalization, 5:04
   for emphasis, 19:08
   punctuating, 5:05-06
   and logic (parallelism), 5:07
calendar, 14:05
Commas, 3:01-28, 4:01-05, 4:09-10, 18:29
   with cities and countries, 3:23
   with cities and states, 3:23
   with dates and days of the week,
      3:19-22, 7:25
   with independent clauses joined by
      coordinating conjunctions, 3:02-06, 3:27,
      4:02-04, 4:07
   with interrupters, 3:16-23, 3:27, 13:27
   with introductory elements, 3:07-10,
      3:18, 3:27, 4:09-10
   with *Jr*, *Sr*, *III,* and *Esq*, 9:05
   with numbers, 25
   optional, 3:03, 3:08, 3:12, 3:27-28, 4:09-10,
   and (closing) quotation marks, 3:24
   and sentence variety, 18:29
   after *then*, 4:10
   with three or more items in a series,
      3:11-12, 3:27, 4:05
   with two or more adjectives preceding a noun,
      3:13-14, 3:27
   with *which*, 13:27
Company Policy and saying *no*, 20:20
Comparative and superlative degrees, 10:01-10
   combined comparatives and
      superlatives, 10:09
   comparing two things, 10:10
   irregular, 10:07
   -ly words, 10:06
   nearly, more nearly, most nearly, 10:08
   none possible, 10:08
   one-syllable, 10:02
   three or more syllables, 10:04
   two-syllable, 10:03, 10:05
Compound adjectives (see Hyphenating
   compound adjectives)
Congratulatory notes, 21:27-28
Conjunctive adverbs, 4:08, 5:02
consensus of opinion, 13:13
Coordinating conjunctions, 3:02-06, 3:27, 4:02-04, 4:07
   beginning a sentence with, 4:04
Countries, punctuation with, 3:23
criteria—criterion, 11:13

Dashes, 5:01, 5:08-10
   with capitalization in titles, 6:14
   following introductory lists, 5:08-10
data—datum, 1:04, 11:13, page 166
Dates, 12-15
   with days of the week, 3:20
   international format, 3:22, 7:14
   punctuating, 3:19-22
De-emphasizing information, 19:11, 20:14-16
Degrees (see Comparative and
   superlative degrees)
Demonstrative pronouns
   dangling, 18:15
   them, used as, 2:10
Dependent clauses, 8:05, 8:08-09, 13:27
Diagonal (/), 7:15, 18:10
Dialects, 23:04-05
   Scotch-Irish, page 165
   Southern, page 165
A Dictionary of Modern English Usage
   (*Fowler*), 24:06
differ with, 13:15
different from—different than, 13:14
Dismissals, 21:22-26
Dollar symbol, 7:19, 7:24, 9:07
done—already, 13:16
Double negatives, 18:34
each other—one another, 13:11
effect, as a noun or verb, 13:03-04
Emphasizing information, 13:25, 18:06, 18:30,
   19:01-10, 20:16
   formal methods, 19:02-09
   informal methods, 19:10
Employment applications, 21:02-08
enough, singular or plural, 1:03
ensure, 13:08
Esq, 9:04-05
every day—everyday, 13:17
everyone—every one, 13:07
Exclamation marks and quotations, 3:25
farther—further, 13:18
February, 14:07
fewer, 13:06
Fowler (see *A Dictionary of Modern
   English Usage,* 24:06)
French, 8:06, 14:01
further, 13:18
German, 14:01, 18:14
get, 13:25, 18:35, 18:38
Gobbledygook, 17:06, 18:01, 18:38

Good-news letters, 20:02-10, 20:12, 20:27
Good news versus bad news,
    organization, 20:12
Grammatical courtesy, 2:03
Gregg (see *The Gregg Reference Manual*)
The Gregg Reference Manual (Sabin), page iii,
    4:08, 6:13, 9:11, 15:20, 24:04, 24:06
Headings, capitalization in, 6:13-16
Hyphenated words in titles, 6:15
Hyphenating compound adjectives, 15:01-22
    compound complement adjectives, 15:12, 15:16
    exceptions, 15:13-20
    following a verb, 15:03-05, 15:12
    with numbers, 15:09, 15:18
    preceding a noun, 15:07
    with prefixes, 15:11, 15:24
    with *self* and *ex*, 15:11
    with *well* and *ill*, 15:10, 15:19
Idioms, 2:11, 8:06
ill with hyphenated adjectives, 15:10, 15:19
Improving your English, 23:01-05
    correcting bad habits, 23:02
    developing the right attitude, 23:04
    reprogramming your behavior, 23:03
Inc, 9:04-05
Independent clauses, 3:01-11, 3:27, 4:02, 4:06-08, 5:02-03,
    5:09-10, 8:05, 18:29, 18:37
insure, 13:08
Interview follow-up notes, 21:09-11
irregardless, 13:19
it's—its, 12:06-08, 14:09
Jargon, 17:07, 18:01, 18:08-10
Journalistic style, page ii, 3:12, 4:04
Jr, 9:04-05
lay, 13:28-31
Lecturing the reader, 20:21
lend–loan, 13:20
less—fewer, 13:06
Letter length, 18:26, 21:06
Letters, memorandums, and e-mails, 20:01-26,
    21:01-30
    bad-news, 19:11, 20:11-26
    congratulatory notes, 21:27-28
    dismissals, 21:22-26
    employment applications, 21:02-08
    good-news, 20:02-10, 20:12
    good news versus bad news,
        organization, 20:12
    interview follow-up notes, 21:09-11
    neutral-news, 20:02-10
    recommendations, 21:12-18

resignations, 21:19-21
résumé cover letters, 21:02-08
saying *NO*, 20:11-26
thank-you letters, 21:29-30
lie—lay, 13:28-31
Lists, 5:02-10, 19:08
loan—lend, 13:20
Margins
    ragged right, 18:36
    wide, 18:36
majority, 13:21
matrix—matrices, 11:13
may, 13:12
media—medium, 1:04
Memorandums (see Letters, memorandums and
    e-mails)
Memorandum subject lines, 6:14-17
Merriam-Webster's Collegiate Dictionary,
    page iii, 6:13, 9:11, 15:19, 15:22, 24:02-03, page 166
Money, 7:19-26, 9:07
money—monies, 18:23
most, singular or plural, 1:03
Neutral-news letters, 20:02-10
NO, how to say, 20:11-26
none, singular or plural, 1:03
Normans, 8:06
Noun piles, 18:14
number
    misuse of, 13:05
    singular or plural, 1:03
Numbers, 7:01-27
    approximations, 7:02, 7:08
    commas with, 7:25-26
    dates, 7:12-15, 7:25
    decimals, 7:26
    fractions, 7:09-11
    money, 7:19-26
    with *percent*, 7:07
    plurals of, 7:27
    spelled or written as numerals, 7:01-10,
        7:19-20, 7:22
    time, expressions of, 7:16-18
one (the pronoun), 18:18
one another, 13:11
Oxford English Dictionary, 24:09, page 166
Paragraph length, 18:05-06, 18:36, 19:06, 19:11, 20:14,
    20:15, 20:27
part, singular or plural, 1:03
party—person, 13:22
Passing the buck, 20:20
Passive voice, 17:01, 17:03-07
    abuse of, 17:06-07, 18:19, 22:02

percent
- hyphenation, 15:17
- with numerals, 7:07
- singular or plural, 1:03

people→persons, 13:23

Periods
- with abbreviations, 9:09, 9:11
- in columns, 5:05-06
- instead of semicolons, 4:06-09
- with quotation marks, 3:24

person→party, 13:22

persons→people, 13:23

Personal titles and positions, 6:02-05

Plain English, 18:21-23

plenty, singular or plural, 1:03

Plurals, 11:01-13
- of abbreviations, 9:09
- of compound nouns, 11:11-12
- irregular, 11:13
- of nouns ending with *o*, 11:07-08
- of nouns ending with *s, ch, sh, x,* or *z*, 11:02-05
- of nouns ending with *st*, 11:06
- of nouns ending with *y*, 11:09-10
- of numbers, 7:27
- of peoples names ending with *s, ch, sh, x,* or *z*, 11:03-05
- pomposity, 18:23
- possessives of plural nouns, 12:02-03
- pronouns that can be singular or plural, 1:03, 2:11
- without *s*, 1:04, 11:13
- *their* with singular pronouns, 2:11
- uncommon, 1:04, 18:23

Pomposity, 8:06, 13:27, 17:01, 18:01, 18:08-24

Possessives, 12:01-13
- of abbreviations, 9:10
- of *it*, 12:06-07, 14:09
- joint possession (by two or more people or things), 12:13-14
- of names that end with *x* or *z*, 12:15
- of nouns that end with *s*, 12:04, 12:10
- of plural nouns that do not end with *s*, 12:03
- of pronouns, 12:04-07, 14:09
- pronouns with *-ing* words, 2:07-09
- *their*, 14:09, 14:11
- *their* with singular pronouns, 2:11-15

Predicate adjective, 15:03

Prefixes, hyphenating, 15:24

Prepositional phrases and subject-verb agreement, 1:02-03

Prepositions
- for avoiding noun piles, 18:14
- capitalization in titles, 6:13-14
- ending sentences with, 8:03, 18:12
- with *whom*, 8:02
- with *whomever*, 8:08-09

principal→principle, 13:24

Professional titles, 6:02-05

Pronouns, 2:01-15
- with *as* and *than*, 2:04
- confused choice when other words interfere, 2:02
- demonstrative, dangling, 18:15
- grammatical courtesy, 2:03
- indefinite, 1:03, 12:04
- with *-ing* words, 2:07-09
- personal, 12:06-08, 14:09
- possessive, 2:07-09, 12:04-07, 14:09, 14:11
- reflexive, 2:05-06, 18:16
- singular or plural, 1:03, 2:11
- testing for complement adjectives, 15:05
- *their* used with singular pronouns like *everyone*, 2:11-15
- using and avoiding first-person pronouns, 18:02, 18:38, 20:15
- using and avoiding second-person pronouns, 18:03, 20:04, 20:18

Proofreading, 14:01, 18:25, 22:01-10, 23:04
- goofy reading, 22:05
- involving other people, 22:09
- letting time pass, 22:06
- straightedge, 22:04
- using computers, 22:02

Question marks and quotations, 3:25

Quotation marks, 6:17
- punctuation with, 3:24-26

real(ly)→very→get, 13:25, 18:35

Recipe English, 18:20

Recommendation letters, 21:12-18

Redundancies, 7:17, 13:25, 18:32-34

Resignation letters, 21:19-21

rest, singular or plural, 1:03

Résumé cover letters, 21:02-08

Résumés, 9:02, 21:02, 22:10

Roman numerals with names, 9:05

Scotch-Irish dialect, page 165

Semicolons, 4:01-11
- with conjunctive adverbs, 4:08-10
- with independent clauses joined by coordinating conjunctions, 4:02-04

with independent clauses not joined
by coordinating conjunctions, 4:06-07
with items in a series, 3:15, 4:05
with quotation marks, 3:26
with transitional expressions, 4:08-10
Sentence length, 18:04-05, 18:28, 18:37, 19:05
Sentence variety, 18:28-29
separate, 14:10
set, 13:28-30
Shakespeare, William, 13:01
shall, 18:13
sit—set, 13:28-30
slash (/) (see Diagonal)
so and *so that*, 3:06, 3:27
some, singular or plural, 1:03
Southern Dialect, page 165
Spanish, 14:01
species—species, 1:04
Spelling, 14:01-16
frequently misspelled words, 14:02-12
guidelines, 14:13-16
and pronunciation, 14:01
spelling checkers, 22:02
of symbols, 9:07
Sr, 9:04-05
States, punctuation with, 3:23
Subject lines (memorandum),
capitalization in, 6:13-16
Subject-verb agreement, 1:01-07
with compound subjects (two or more
people or things), 1:05
confused by prepositional phrases, 1:02
controlled by prepositional phrases, 1:03
when subjects follow verbs, 1:06
with unusual plurals, 1:04
with verbs that end with *st*, 1:07
Subjunctive mood, 16:01-10
determining the correct verb form, 16:05-06
had had, 16:10
have instead of *of*, 16:08
with *if-would* sentences, 16:04
might could, 16:09
were instead of *was*, 16:07
with wishes, 16:02
Superlatives (see Comparatives and superlatives)
sure—surely, 13:26
syllabi—syllabus, 1:04

Symbols, 9:07
cent, 7:23-24
monetary, including dollar, 7:19, 7:24, 9:07
Thank-you letters, 21:29-30
thank you, thoughtless, 20:08
that—which, 13:27, 18:11-12
their with singular pronouns, 2:11-15
their—there—they're, 14:11
them, misuse of, 2:10
then
no comma after, 4:10
redundant, 18:33
Time, expressions of, 7:16-18
Titles
of people, 6:02-05
of presentations, 6:17
of software
of written works, 6:13-17
to—too, 14:12
total, singular or plural, 1:03
Transitional expressions, 4:08-10, 5:02
Underline, 6:17, 19:10
Understanding English Grammar (Kolln), 24:07
The understood *you*, 1:01, 3:01, 3:05
Variety
sentence, 18:04, 18:28-29
word, 18:30-35
very, 13:25
Webster, Noah, page 166
Webster's Third New International Dictionary,
page 166
well, with hyphenated adjectives, 15:10, 15:19
which, 13:27, 18:11-12
White space, 18:36, 19:06
who—whom, 8:01-07, 8:11, 8:13
at the beginning of a dependent clause, 8:05
with prepositions, 8:02-03
without prepositions, 8:04
with *to be* verbs, 8:06-07
versus than and which, 13:27
who—whose—who's, 12:09
whoever—whomever, 8:08-09, 8:12
whosever, 12:09
Word variety, 18:30
Words, culling unnecessary, 18:27
You-oriented letters, memorandums, and e-mails
18:03,
20:04, 20:18
you, understood, 1:01, 3:01, 3:05
your—you're, 14:08

NOTES

Printed in the United States
143932LV00002B/4/P